T0312820

THE BIG BOOK

OF

ZELDA

THE UNOFFICIAL GUIDE TO

BREATH OF THE WILD AND
THE LEGEND OF ZELDA

This book is book is available in quantity at special discounts for your group or organization. For further information, contact:

Triumph Books LLC
814 North Franklin Street
Chicago, Illinois 60610
Phone: (312) 337-0747
www.triumphbooks.com

Printed in U.S.A.
ISBN: 978-1-62937-523-6

Interior design by Patricia Frey
Cover design by Preston Pisellini

Contents

CHAPTER 1

What Is The Legend of Zelda?

Released in North America in 1987, The Legend of Zelda marked an important moment in the history of video games. It showed that a game with a real sense of exploration and adventure could be enjoyed even on a game console as simple as the 8-bit Nintendo Entertainment System.

Players took on the role of Link, exploring the open world of Hyrule, fighting monsters, discovering secrets, using tools, solving puzzles, and getting lost in a video game experience unlike anything before it. Hyrule felt alive, and Link's journey felt important, even though there wasn't much of a story.

The game led to many sequels, and each has changed the way video games are designed up to this day. Nearly every successful modern video game designer points to The Legend of Zelda as an influence and there's a good reason why—The Legend of Zelda is one of the best video games ever made.

The Development

Shigeru Miyamoto is credited as Zelda's creator and often said the exploration of the woods and caves near his childhood

home as a boy was the primary inspiration for the game's story. Miyamoto's first idea for Zelda was a multiplayer game where two players could design dungeons for one another to explore. The people at Nintendo decided that the best part of the experience was exploring the dungeons. From there, Miyamoto and the rest of Nintendo's development team began building a game focusing on the idea of dungeon exploration.

During development, the experience made its way above ground. The dungeons were incorporated into the overworld of Hyrule, and a story about a boy named Link

on a journey to save a princess named Zelda began to take shape.

Today, The Legend of Zelda is in the safe hands of producer and sometimes director, Eiji Aonuma. Aonuma joined the franchise by working on Ocarina of Time, and was credited as the director of its sequel, The Legend of Zelda: Majora's Mask. Aonuma oversees The Legend of Zelda, with guidance from its original creator, Shigeru Miyamoto.

Alongside Miyamoto and Aonuma, a number of other prominent Nintendo developers have been involved with Zelda. Takashi Tezuka has been with Nintendo since 1984 and has served as writer, director, co-director, and designer on an assortment of Nintendo games, including most of the early Mario and Zelda games. Tezuka was instrumental in the development of the original Zelda, Link to the Past, and Link's Awakening.

Yoshiaki Koizumi's first job after getting hired with Nintendo was putting together the manual for Link to the Past, but he quickly moved into more prominent roles, penning the strange story of Link's Awakening, working on Ocarina of Time, and coming up with the core time travel mechanic of Majora's Mask.

Hiromasa Shikata, a comparably young designer at Nintendo, served as director on Link Between Worlds and the multiplayer follow-up, Tri Force Heroes. Before that, he worked on the world layout for Ocarina of Time, Majora's Mask, and Wind Waker.

More recently Hidemaro Fujibayashi has served as director of the Zelda games alongside Aonuma's watchful producer eye. Fujibayashi got his start in the video game industry working on PlayStation and Sega Saturn games, but started work on Zelda with the Oracle of Ages and Seasons games. He directed those games and went on to direct Minish Cap, Skyward Sword, and the recent Breath of the Wild.

The Story

Through the franchise's 30 years, the core story of each entry has basically stayed the same: The Legend of Zelda follows a young warrior named Link who must save a princess named Zelda and defeat the evil Ganon. The Triforce, a powerful three-piece object that represents Courage, Wisdom, and Power, is also usually part of the game. When its three pieces are combined it has the power to grant its owner a wish. Link, Zelda, and Ganon sometimes represent the Courage, Wisdom, and Power attributes of the Triforce.

Sometimes the same Link and Zelda will move between games for direct sequels, but often, each game represents a new generation of Link and Zelda as they fight the forces of evil. The same goes for Ganon, though he is not always the villain, nor does the Triforce always play an important role.

The main things that set each entry apart is who stands in Link's way, the world he is exploring, what tools he uses to make his way to Zelda, and finally, what type of controller you're holding in your hand while you join Link on his journey.

CHAPTER 2

What Makes a Zelda Game?

There are many thing that define a Zelda game, but there is no outline of rules that say a Zelda game must have these things in order to be considered a true Zelda experience. If that were the case, then Nintendo would break its own rules often. But here are many elements that appear in almost every Zelda game.

The Main Characters

Link

The star, the hero, and the character everyone thinks is named Zelda. Despite being the main character, the game is not named after him, which has caused confusion since the release of the original Zelda 30 years ago. He's a skilled warrior, problem solver, and frequently a talented musician.

He is often represented as an orphan without family, but sometimes he does have a caretaker in the form of an uncle, grandmother, or some other family member or friend. He is rarely seen without his green tunic and hat, sword, and shield. He represents the Triforce of Courage and has never had a voice outside of the grunts and shouts that accompany combat and movement.

His name is meant to represent a connection between the player and the world. He is the "link" that connects the player to the game. His name, however, can be chosen by the player. Whatever name players enter in the beginning the game is the one non-player characters will use when referring to him.

Zelda

Zelda is the focus of Link's journey. He must save Zelda. In the early games Zelda was not much more than a damsel in distress. As the storytelling of the games' consoles and technology improved, however, she has become more than just a woman waiting for her hero.

While Link has basically worn his famous green outfit since the beginning, Zelda's look has changed quite a bit over the years. She often wears a crown and a pink dress, but in The Legend of Zelda: The Wind Waker, she was actually a pirate princess and didn't look like royalty at all. In The Legend of Zelda: Ocarina of Time, Zelda adopts a secret identity and helps Link throughout the game without him realizing who she is until the end.

Shigeru Miyamoto has said that he borrowed Zelda's name from the wife of author F. Scott Fitzgerald, Zelda Fitzgerald. She represents the Triforce of Wisdom.

Ganon

Sometimes his name is Ganon; sometimes his name is Ganondorf; sometimes he is a pig beast; sometimes he is a human that turns into a giant pig beast. He's not the villain in every Zelda game, but he usually is, even if that isn't clear until the very end.

He represents the Triforce of Power, and stealing Zelda is always part of the process toward acquiring the Triforce. His form changes from game to game, but he usually wears dark clothes and has red hair. Even when he takes on his pig beast form, he usually retains his red hair.

His characterization and voice in the games is usually limited to threats against Link or talking about his plans. Often he is the only male of the Gerudo tribe of women.

In addition to his Ganon or Ganondorf name, on at least one occasion he had the last name Dragmire. He is also sometimes referred to as Great King of Evil or the Dark Lord.

The Secondary Characters

Impa

Present from the very first game, Impa is a character that often gives Link an overview of what to expect over the course of the rest of the game. She imparts knowledge to Link, which is where her name comes from. She does not appear in every game, but when she does she often serves a crucial role in helping Link along his journey. She is typically a member of the Sheikah Tribe, a tribe that is sworn to protect the Hyrule royal family.

Epona

Link's faithful horse, Epona has appeared in many Zelda adventures. In her first appearance in Ocarina of Time, Link wins her in a race, stealing her from Ingo, Epona's caretaker. You can call her to your side and she even fights alongside you sometimes. In Twilight Princess you can give Epona a customized name.

The King of Hyrule

The King of Hyrule typically appears in Zelda games as the father of Zelda and the king of Hyrule. In early games, he would only appear in the backstory, but more recent releases like Wind Waker and Breath of the Wild feature him as a prominent character requesting Link's help in rescuing his daughter.

The Golden Goddesses

Crucially important to the history of Hyrule and the creation of the world in which the Zelda games take place, Din the Goddess of Power, Nayru the Goddess of Wisdom, and Farore the Goddess of Courage together are the Golden Goddesses. In some adventures, they are credited with creating the Triforce. In others, they are credited with crafting the world. And in some, they appear as characters that Link can speak and interact with.

Skull Kid

Skull Kid has only appeared in two Zelda games (though a character similar to Skull Kid does appear in Twilight Princess), but his impact on the series is undeniable. He serves as the main antagonist of Majora's Mask

and wears the mask throughout the game. He's mischievous and intimidating, but also sympathetic.

Tingle

Tingle first appeared in Majora's Mask as a fairy-obsessed man who refuses to grow up, much to his father's dismay. He sells Link maps in Majora's Mask, but proved to be so popular that he has now become one of Zelda's most celebrated side characters. Not only has he appeared in multiple Zelda games after his introduction (he was especially prominent in The Wind Waker), but he had a pair of spinoff games that told

his own strange story. Typically dressed in a green, full-body leotard with red underwear, Tingle is one of the most endearing but strangest characters in the world of Zelda.

Beedle

Beedle is a merchant who first appeared in The Wind Waker, but has appeared in nearly every Zelda game since. He is instantly recognizable for his long nose, distinct haircut, and his enthusiastic "Thank you!" every time you buy something from him. In The Skyward Sword, he was also an avid bug collector, which accounted for a large side quest.

Beedle

Wow! We meet again! It seems that sharing space is our destiny.

The Worlds

Hyrule

Most of Link's adventures take place in the land of Hyrule. Zelda is the princess of Hyrule, and Ganon seeks to take over Hyrule. Link has left Hyrule on occasion to explore neighboring worlds like Termina in Majora's Mask or Hytopia in Tri Force Heroes. Hyrule is home to many locations like Death Mountain—a volcano with a smoke ring around its peak—and the Lost Woods, a complicated maze that holds many secrets.

Termina

The world of Termina is a long horse ride away from Hyrule, if the opening of Majora's Mask is any indication. Some believe it is a creation of Skull Kid's imagination, aided by the magic of the Majora's Mask. It is home to Clock Town, a normal town surrounded by a coast, a swamp, a canyon, and a wintery

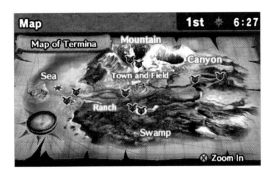

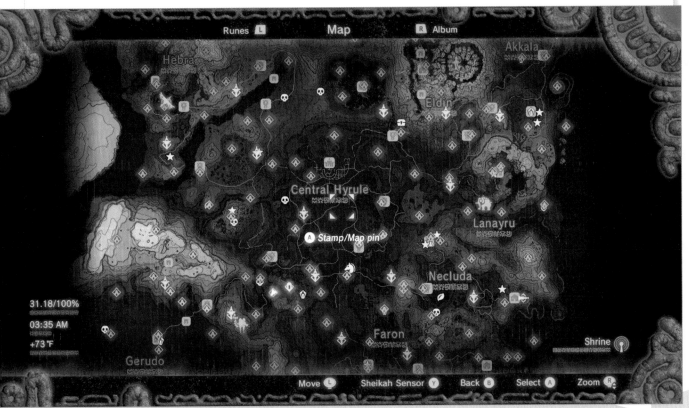

forest. In Majora's Mask, Link relives the same three days exploring Termina, learning about its residents, and preventing the moon from crashing into the world.

Koholint Island

Koholint is another world that may or may not truly exist depending on which Zelda theories you subscribe to. Link crashes in Koholint in the Game Boy's Link's Awakening after his boat gets caught in a violent storm. Koholint is completely disconnected from Hyrule, and features a strange cast of characters inspired by the early 1990s TV show, *Twin Peaks*.

Lorule

In A Link Between Worlds, Link visits the land of Lorule. It's the dark opposite of Hyrule and features twisted duplicates of the locations and characters seen in Hyrule. It is ruled by Princess Hilda (Zelda's opposite), who is doing

all she can to restore her world, which has been shrouded in darkness.

Labrynna and Holodrum

The Game Boy title Oracle of Ages takes place in Labryanna and Oracle of Seasons takes place in Holodrum. Both lands are far from Hyrule, but Link does meet Hylians in both worlds.

Hytopia

Featured in Tri Force Heroes, Hytopia is a world unusually obsessed with fashion and clothing. Among the worlds Link visits during the course of his many adventures, Hytopia may be the one he explores the least. Most of the game takes place in the connected Drablands.

The Music

The music of Zelda is as important as the look of the games. During Link's adventures, he usually uses some sort of instrument.

Written by Koji Kondo, who also created the music for Super Mario Bros., Zelda's music has become famous and instantly recognizable. The first game was planned to use Maurice Ravel's Boléro, but when that was not an option as it was not yet a public domain piece of music, Kondo composed original music for the game.

The themes he created for the original game still appear in The Legend of Zelda today, as Kondo continues to create the soundtrack in cooperation with other composers.

Link's Weapons and Tools

Every Zelda adventure features items that only appear in its game that are used to solve specific puzzles, but there are many that appear in every game.

The Master Sword: This sword is often the only weapon that can defeat Ganondorf, and Link is often the only one who can use it. It must usually be removed from a stone, like the sword of the King Arthur legend, and has a blue handle. In Skyward Sword, the Master Sword was given a personality and voice in the form of Fi.

The Hylian shield: Link goes through many shields over the course of even a single adventure, but the Hylian shield, which is blue and features Hylian symbols and imagery, is his protection of choice.

The bow and arrow: An important weapon in any fantasy story, Link uses the bow and arrow to solve puzzles as well as fight enemies. When Zelda joins the battle, she uses the bow and arrow as her weapon of choice. It can also take on fire, ice, and light abilities.

The boomerang: An important weapon that can be used to stun enemies but does not use ammunition. It sometimes takes on additional magic properties, like wind, as it did in Twilight Princess.

The bomb: Being able to blow up stuff like walls and enemies is important.

The bombchu: Being able to place a bomb on the ground that scurries off to blow up something in the distance is equally important.

The hookshot: An important tool for navigation and movement, the hookshot allows Link to pull himself to faraway locations, or pull enemies toward him.

The bottle: Bottles are containers that can hold potions, life-giving fairies, and many other useful objects or items. Link usually carries more than one.

Musical instruments: Link always enjoys music, but his favorite instrument changes from game to game. He has used a flute, a pan flute, an ocarina, a harp, a conductor's baton, drums, and even a guitar.

Magical rods: Link isn't always able to use a magical rod, but when he does, he is able to fire off fireballs, ice attacks, and more. Usually, the rod is connected to specific element.

The slingshot: Young Link, on occasion, will find a slingshot to fire off limited projectiles. It's never as strong as the bow and is usually abandoned once Link is able to fire an arrow.

The bug net: Link is usually a bug collector, depending on the game, but the main advantage of the bug net is to capture fairies, which brings us to…

Fairies: Link can hold fairies, typically in bottles, that will instantly bring him back to

life the moment he runs out of hearts. They are among his most valuable healing items.

Bracelets and gauntlets: Link is capable of wielding a powerful sword and carrying around a bag with an absurd amount of items, but that doesn't mean he can't stand to be a little stronger. Sometimes it's a gauntlet, sometimes it's a bracelet, but both allow Link to lift larger and heavier items, like rocks, or in the case of Ocarina of Time, gigantic pillars of stone.

Heart pieces and containers: Link typically begins every game with three hearts, but he can get more hearts by defeating bosses, or collecting heart pieces in the world. More hearts means Link can take more damage, making him stronger.

The paraglider: This is a very recent item in the Zelda canon, but it has appeared in other forms in previous Zelda games. In The Wind Waker it was a giant Deku Leaf. In Skyward Sword, it was the Sailcloth, but the purpose is the same—let Link glide from high heights. Breath of the Wild makes the greatest use of the item and is instrumental to exploring the game's massive open world.

The Enemies

Link fights many enemies of all sizes on his adventures, but there are a few bad guys that Link has been fighting for lifetimes and it's likely he always will. This is far from all of the enemies Link faces, but these are some of the ones that always seem to make an appearance.

Moblins: The most standard of standard enemy, millions of moblins have been felled by Link's sword. Sometimes they are called bokoblins, but they are always weaker, goblin-like enemies that Link fights early, and throughout, nearly every Zelda game.

Beamos: Something between a cyclops and a statue, the Beamos keeps Link in its sights and fires lasers at him.

ChuChu: These adorable slime creatures can do a lot of damage to Link if he's not cautious as they can electrocute him.

Keese: Bats are the most annoying enemies in all of video games, and Keese keep that reputation alive and strong.

Octoroks: The Octorok has fought Link since the very first game. These octopus-like creatures shoot rocks at Link after they poke their heads out of the water.

Gibdo: The Gibdo has appeared in nearly every Zelda game. It's a mummy-creature that Link can set on fire.

Like Like: The Like Like eats Link, spits him out, and steals his items. Sometimes he might only take a few rupees, but sometimes he takes far more important items.

Stalfos: These enemies are skeletons. It seems like every fantasy game or fantasy fiction has to have them. Sometimes they carry swords and shields, but often they just chuck their own bones at Link.

Tektite: This creature has spider-like qualities, but only has four legs. It leaps into the air to attack, and can navigate the surface of the water.

Wallmaster: These giant hands are among Zelda's most terrifying enemies. They can rarely be fought, and instead drop from the ceiling to steal Link away. They show up in dungeons and will appear when Link stands still for too long.

Wizzrobe: Sometimes spelled with a single 'z', Wizzrobes specialize in throwing magic attacks at Link.

Hinox: Based on the cyclops, Hinox are super powerful enemies that are typically seen late in the game. In Breath of the Wild, they are massive minibosses that can be encountered in the open world.

Lynel: Like the Hinox, Lynel are typically not seen until much later in the game. They are centaur creatures who are quick to take down Link if he's not prepared.

CHAPTER 3

The Legend of Zelda (NES, 1986)

The game that started it all, The Legend of Zelda was released in 1986, just one year after the launch of the NES in North America. The console came packed with Super Mario Bros., and much of the console's success is thanks to the plumber brothers. But The Legend of Zelda showed players how open, rewarding, and fun an interactive video game world could be. Players loved the open nature of the game. The Legend of Zelda presented a world that felt alive and dangerous, and how it was explored was up to the player.

The game is played from the overhead perspective. Players looked down on Link from above, directing his movements and combat in a large open world. In the beginning Link is completely powerless without any offensive or defensive items. There is a cave directly north that can be entered to receive a sword from an old man who famously says, "It's dangerous to go alone! Take this." With his sword in hand, Link can then explore the world.

Zelda, alongside games like Ultima and Hydlide, are among the first to be considered open world. Zelda was not broken into levels, and though parts of the world are blocked off until the player achieves certain

milestones, it is a consistent, interconnected series of locations. The player never leaves the game between areas.

The original game set many of the standards The Legend of Zelda franchise continues to follow today. In order to progress, players have to track down a collection of dungeons. Each dungeon is a series of puzzles that ends with a boss fight.

New items discovered in the world help with completing each dungeon, fighting enemies, and navigating the world.

The Legend of Zelda was not just the first Zelda game, but also one of the first games to offer the ability to save. This meant players could pick up right where they left off from their previous Zelda play session without having to start from the beginning every time. This helped make the world of Hyrule more believable, as not having to restart the game over and over made it feel as though the world was alive.

The Story

By today's standards, the original Zelda's story is pretty basic. You are a little dude in a green tunic with a sword who has to fight monsters, and in the end you save a princess. This is the amount of story in the actual game, but the instruction booklet offered some more details.

An evil pig demon named Ganon has invaded the kingdom of Hyrule and stolen the Triforce of Power. To prevent him from stealing the Triforce of Wisdom, Princess Zelda splits it into eight pieces. Ganon kidnaps her after she does this, but not before she is able to send her nursemaid, Impa, out into the world to find someone capable of saving the kingdom. Link runs into Impa as she is being attacked by Ganon's henchmen and saves her. She asks Link to take up the mantle of hero and save Princess Zelda, and that's where the game begins. In the end, Link is able to bring the fragments back together to form the Triforce of Wisdom and defeat Ganon.

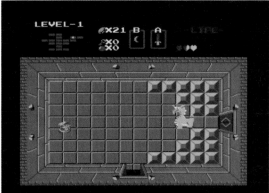

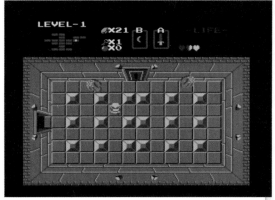

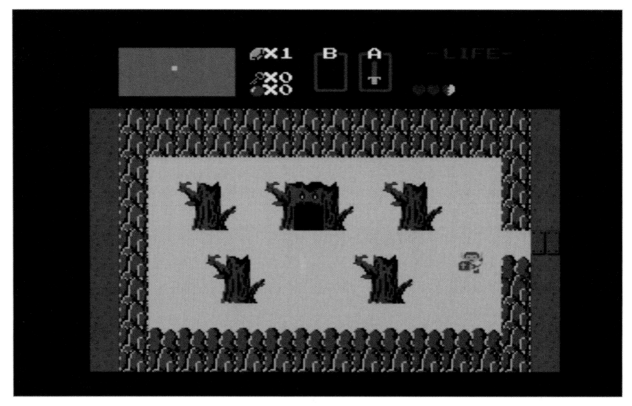

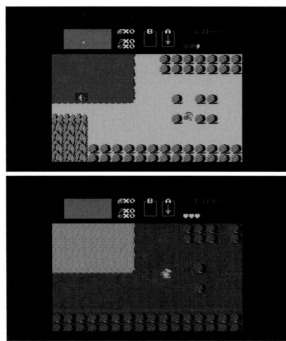

The Items

The first Legend of Zelda set a standard for Link and his long-term relationship with items. The sword is necessary in order to fight monsters, but for every other task in the world, there are items. The Legend of Zelda is the first place Link found and used a bow and arrow, a boomerang, bombs, magic rods, and more. It's also home to the raft, which allows Link to float on the water in order to make it to out of reach islands.

The Re-releases

Even though Nintendo likes to remake its games, the original Legend of Zelda has never received a proper remake. It has, however, been re-released on a number of platforms other than the NES. You can find the game on Game Boy Advance and GameCube, as well as the Wii, 3DS, and Wii U Virtual Consoles. These versions of the game are all straightforward copies that do not include any changes or upgrades from the game's original 1986 release.

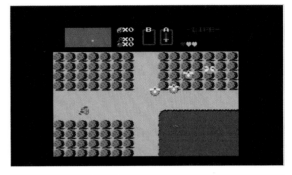

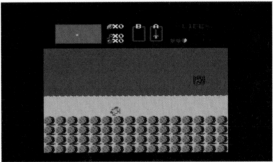

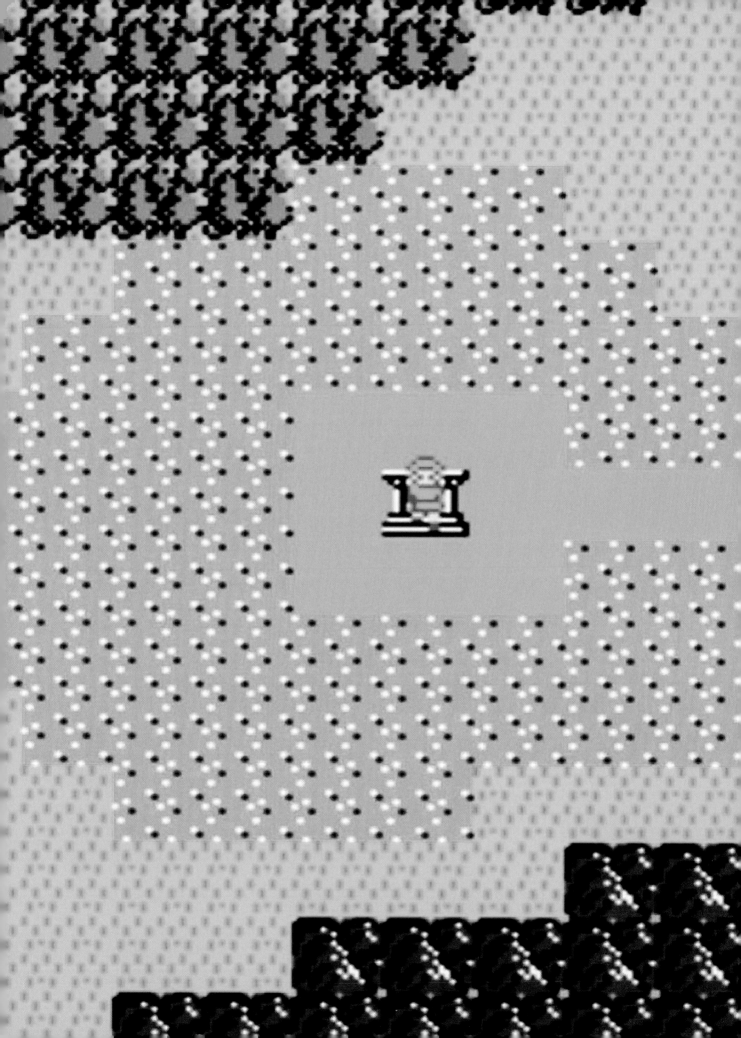

CHAPTER 4

Zelda II: The Adventure of Link (NES, 1988)

To date, the second Zelda game is the only game in the series (not counting spinoffs) that isn't legendary. It is the only mainline Zelda game that does not begin with the three words, "The Legend of…" despite being one of the few direct Zelda sequels. The gameplay in The Adventure of Link is also unlike the first game.

Zelda II splits its gameplay between an overhead view, much like the one seen in The Legend of Zelda, and a side-scrolling action game. Players control Link from above when he is exploring the overworld. While exploring, enemies will appear and

trigger a switch to side-scrolling gameplay for combat. During combat, Link can duck or stand upright while swinging his sword, and he eventually learns to do upward and downward stabbing motions.

The side-scrolling view is also used when Link visits friendly locations. The original Zelda feature some non-player characters (NPCs), but the number and personality of these types in Zelda II is much higher. Link can visit towns, meet the locals, and even perform tasks for them.

Zelda II also uses lives and employs experience points for the first and last time

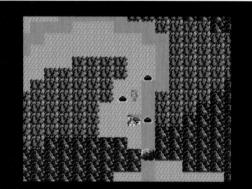

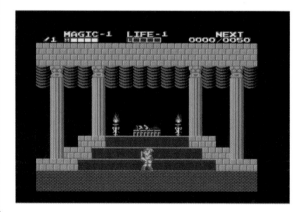

in a Zelda game. Successful combat gives Link points he can distribute between his attack, magic, and life levels in order to increase them. This was very unlike the first game, which based Link's progress in the game simply on the items he found.

Zelda II is a divisive game among fans. It's among the most difficult of the games in the Zelda series and is very different in its structure and gameplay. Despite being fairly different from the rest of the series, it also marked a number of firsts that would continue to appear in follow-up Zelda games. Friendly locations with NPCs Link can talk to, for example, as well as Dark Link, a recurring Zelda enemy, first appeared in Zelda II.

The Story

In general, the Zelda series does not do direct sequels. There are a few, but mostly, each Zelda game represents a new generation of Link playing out a new adventure. Zelda II, however, is one of the few direct sequels to a Zelda game, and features the Link from the first game. This time around, Link discovers a symbol on the back of his hand that resembles the crest of Hyrule. Link shows the symbol to Princess Zelda's nursemaid, Impa, who takes him to the North Castle, where his hand is able to open a door that has been magically sealed for a very long time. Inside the castle is the very first Princess Zelda, who is under a curse that keeps her asleep. She is not the Zelda Link saved in the previous game, but rather the very first Princess Zelda.

Before she was asleep, her dying father passed along secret information about the Triforce of Courage directly to her. Zelda's

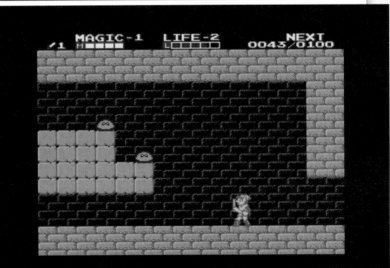

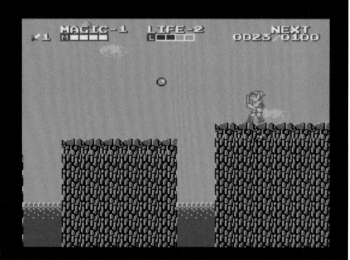

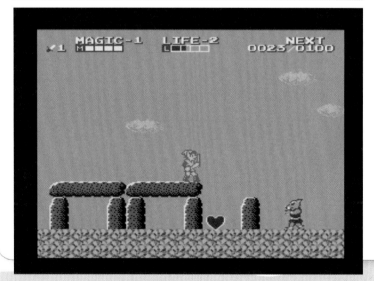

brother wanted to know what she knew, and when she refused to share, he found a wizard who cursed her to sleep. When he realized the princess could never be woken up, the brother felt guilty and decided that all of the kingdom's princesses be named Zelda in her honor.

The symbol on the back of Link's hand identifies him as the hero that can finally awaken her, and the adventure begins. Link must deliver a collection of six crystals to an assortment of statues in the world while fighting Ganon's army, who believes they can bring their leader back to life by sprinkling Link's blood on Ganon's ashes.

The Items

Zelda II has a number of exclusive items that have very specific uses, like the Cross which reveals invisible enemies, the Handy Glove for breaking stones, and the Hammer. Some of these come back in later games, but in different forms. Link has an item that reveals invisible enemies in Ocarina of Time, but it is called the Lens of Truth. One particularly cool item is a pair of boots you can find that allow Link to walk on water.

The Re-releases

Some players really like Zelda II, but many others don't. It was a popular hit when it was released, but Zelda fans today think it doesn't really fit in when looking at the full library of Zelda games. It's much different than other Zelda games, and this could contribute to

the reason Nintendo has never done a full remake of the game.

Like the first Zelda game, it has never received a significant upgrade or remake, but it has been re-released on multiple platforms. The game was given a GBA and GameCube re-release, and some of the game's content was slightly changed. The text was cleaned up a little bit, and Link's death screen, which used to flash with a strobe effect, was toned down. The game is also available on the 3DS, Wii, and Wii U Virtual Consoles.

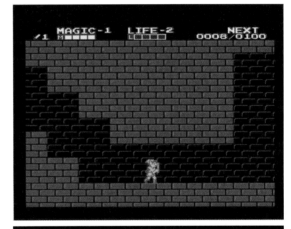

CHAPTER 5

The Legend of Zelda: A Link to the Past (SNES, 1992)

A Link to the Past is considered by many to be the best Zelda game ever made. Every game in the Zelda series has its fans that will say it is the best, but Link to the Past has the most. In Japan the game's subtitle roughly translates to The Triforce of the Gods. In an effort to remove religious references from the game that could be considered controversial in North America, the game's subtitle was changed. It launched about three years after Zelda II and was a fairly early release in the Super Nintendo's library of games. It opens with a 3D model of the Triforce rotating into place. Compared to today's games, the

graphics are not that impressive, but back in 1992 seeing 3D models was mind blowing, and it quickly established that Link to the Past was going to be something special.

For Zelda's first jump to a new generation of consoles, it returned to its roots. Zelda II's split between overhead and side-scrolling gameplay was replaced by a fully overhead perspective, just like the original. Players explored a large, open Hyrule as Link, collecting both new and familiar items. Its gameplay overall was not that different from the original Zelda, but

© 1991, 1992 Nintendo

every aspect from Link's movement to combat was improved.

Link to the Past was the first Zelda game to establish what has now become a common feature of Zelda games: alternate universes. At a certain point in the game, Link is able to move between the standard Hyrule and a dark, twisted Hyrule. The two Hyrules are layed out the same, but feature different color schemes, characters, and enemies, among many other small differences.

Link to the Past features a strange secret room. The room is difficult to access, features a handful of rupees, and contains the text, "My name is Chris Houlihan. This is my top secret room. Keep it between us, okay?" The room was the result of a contest held in *Nintendo Power* magazine where the winner would appear in an upcoming Zelda game.

The Story

Link to the Past is one of the few games where Link has family. It opens with Link's sleeping uncle leaving their home on a rainy night to go save Princess Zelda. A nightmare wakes Link and he goes after his uncle, only to find that he has failed his mission on his way to Zelda's cell. Link takes up his uncle's sword to continue his mission.

Link breaks Zelda out of jail and learns that a wizard named Agahnim is planning to break Ganon out of the Dark World, where he was sent hundreds of years ago. To prevent this Link must rescue the descendants of Seven Sages, which requires he explore Hyrule and its dungeons, solving

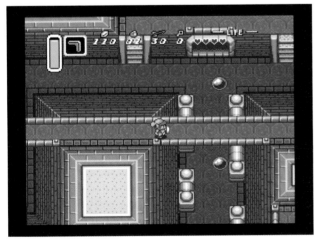
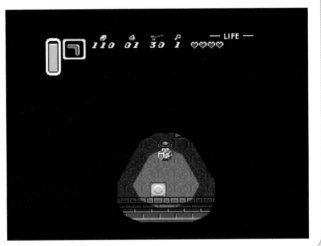

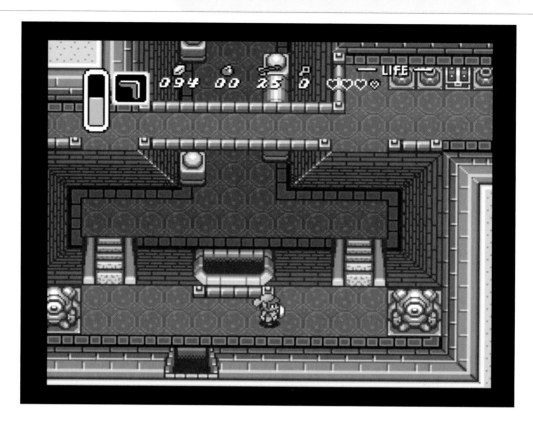

puzzles and finding new items along the way.

The Items

Link finds a number of important items to help him prevent the rise of Ganon. Some are familiar, like the boomerang, and bow and arrow, but there are a few items that would become very important in future games.

Link to the Past marks the first appearance of the hookshot, an item that pulls Link toward objects, and can also be used to pull objects toward him. The item became especially important in the later 3D Zelda games where Link would use the hookshot to climb to high locations.

Link to the Past also marks the first appearance of the very useful glass bottle. When interviewed about the game during development, Zelda's creator Shigeru Miyamoto cited the bottle as being one of Link to the Past's most exciting new elements. The bottle is very simple, but is very valuable. Glass must be very difficult to find in Hyrule, because getting your hands on bottles in any Zelda game is always difficult, and always worth the effort.

The glass bottle lets you hold other items, like health or magic potions, bugs, or even fairies, which grant health to you the moment you die. Allowing players to choose what they wanted to put in bottles let them explore the game in their own way.

The Re-releases

After its Super Nintendo release, Link to the Past wouldn't resurface as a re-release until 2002, on the Game Boy Advance. The Game Boy Advance version of the game featured some very minor changes, like the Pegasus Boot item name being changed to the Pegasus Shoes.

The Game Boy Advance version of the game was a bundle pack that included both Link to the Past in its mostly unchanged original form, and a brand-new game called Four Swords, which was a multiplayer collection of small Zelda dungeons.

Link to the Past is also available on the Wii, Wii U, and New 3DS Virtual Consoles.

THE LEGEND OF ZELDA™

LINK'S AWAKENING

CHAPTER 6

The Legend of Zelda: Link's Awakening (Game Boy 1993)

Link's Awakening is the first Zelda game to appear on a handheld console, and the first to leave behind the legendary princess. It was not based on the typical Zelda story, but still included the familiar gameplay of exploring a large world from the overhead perspective, finding dungeons and items, solving puzzles, and fighting monsters. And it was all done on a smaller scale in shades of green, and not in full color.

The game has an interesting backstory. It started development as a Game Boy port of A Link to the Past, but it quickly became apparent that bringing that game to Nintendo's handheld would not be possible based on the technical disparity between the two platforms. Zelda's creator, Shigeru Miyamoto, was not involved in the early stages of its creation. Instead, Nintendo programmer Kazuaki Morita and designer Takashi Tezuka (who had worked alongside Miyamoto on the previous Zelda games as well as Mario) started work on the game as an after-hours project with a few Nintendo artists. It was inspired, at least to a small degree, by the 1990s television series *Twin Peaks*.

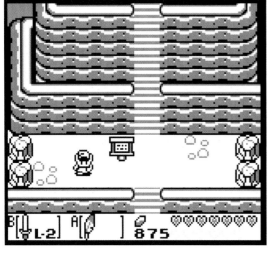

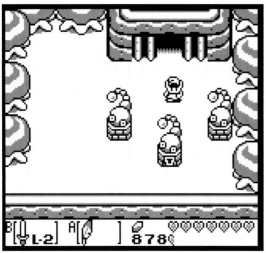

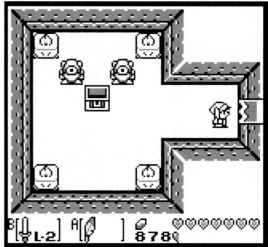

Twin Peaks was a show about a detective working on a case in a small town full of strange characters and unexplainable events. Tezuka wanted Link to follow a similar path. He wanted Link to be out of his element in a land of strange characters, trying to figure out what was going on in a strange new world.

The game was impressive from a technical perspective as it created a full Zelda experience on the Game Boy, something people thought was impossible at the time.

The Story

Link's Awakening begins with Link at sea fighting a violent storm. He loses the battle and ends up washed ashore on Koholint Island, where he is discovered by Marin and taken back to her home to be nursed back to health. Marin is unfamiliar with the world outside of her home and is fascinated by Link's origins.

Link meets a mysterious owl after getting back on his feet who alerts him he must wake the Wind Fish. This means journeying across Koholint Island to eight different dungeons and discovering eight different instruments that must be placed in front

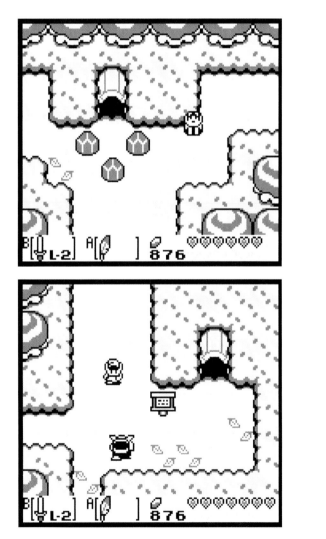

of the giant egg stationed at the peak of a mountain at the island's north.

After finding all of the instruments, Link enters the egg in order to wake the Wind Fish, but first must battle a nightmare that has taken the form of his greatest enemy, Ganon. The game ends with an unlikely twist.

The Items

The usual items all appear in Link's Awakening, including Link's sword, the bow and arrow, and bombs. Maybe the most memorable item from Link's Game Boy adventure is Roc's Feather, which allowed him to leap into the air. From the overhead perspective, Link is able to jump over small holes. When combined with the Pegasus Boots, which allow Link to sprint, he can jump long distances. Roc's Feather is also used during the handful of side-scrolling sections, which played out like shortened Mario-style levels. Link even fights Goombas, from the Mario universe, in some of these sections.

Some of Link's items could also be upgraded to stronger versions. The shield and sword, for example, could be made stronger, as well as a bracelet which Link used to lift heavy rocks and other objects.

The Re-releases

Five years after its original release, Link's Awakening received a re-release for the Game Boy Color called The Legend of Zelda: Link's Awakening DX. This version is in full color, unlike the original game, which could only be played in varying shades of green. Along with the addition of color, DX also added a new optional dungeon. The dungeon played up the new visuals with puzzles and enemies revolving around color. Link could also unlock a red or blue tunic, which gave bonuses to damage and defense. This version also added the option to take screenshots in a few locations, which could be printed out with the Game Boy Printer.

The legend of Zelda: Link's Awakening DX was also released on the 3DS Virtual Console.

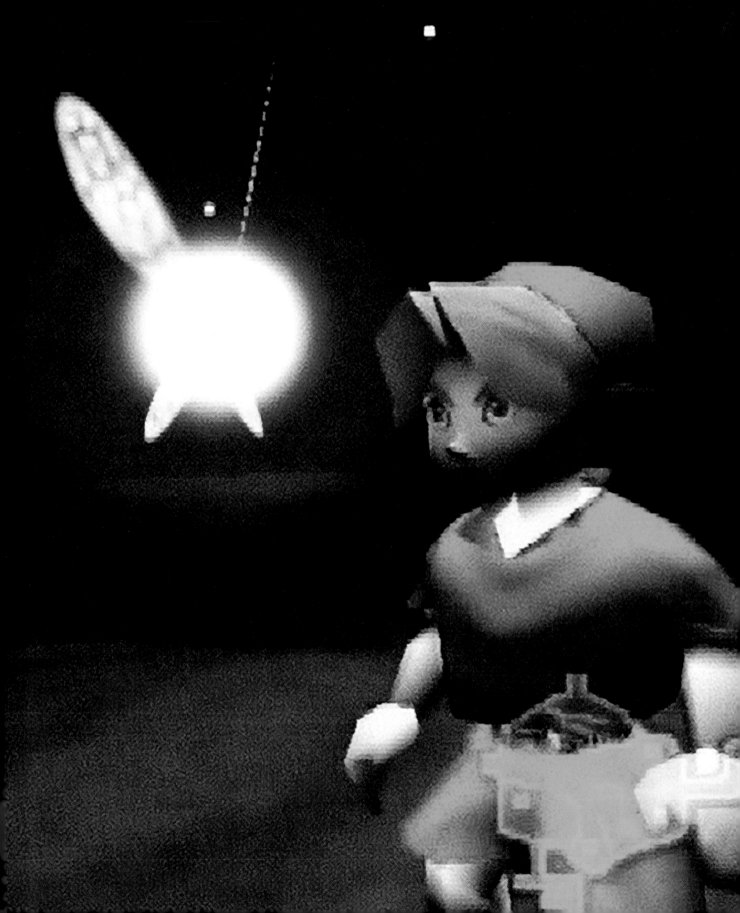

CHAPTER 7

The Legend of Zelda: Ocarina of Time (Nintendo 64, 1998)

Ocarina of Time brought the world of Zelda into the 3D universe and many fans think it and Link to the Past are the best games in the franchise. On Metacritic.com, a website that gathers reviews of video games, movies, and more, Ocarina of Time holds the distinction of being the best-reviewed game ever released. Guinness World Records also called the game the best-reviewed of all time on multiple editions of its world records books. The game was released two years into the Nintendo 64's life cycle and marked the biggest change in the series since Zelda II.

For the most part, the game worked the same way as previous games—you control Link in an open world as he explores, collects items, fights monsters, and solves puzzles on his journey to save Princess Zelda. But the player's viewpoint shifted from overhead to appear directly behind Link. The world and its characters were fully realized in 3D for the first time, giving players a new appreciation for the setting. Early experimentations for the game's development had players exploring an enclosed castle in a similar setup to Super Mario 64 and even playing in the first-person perspective.

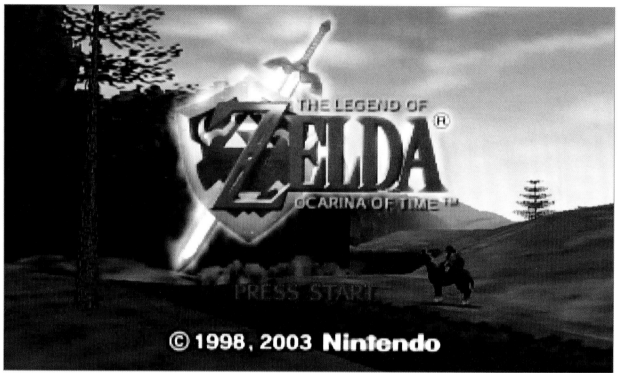

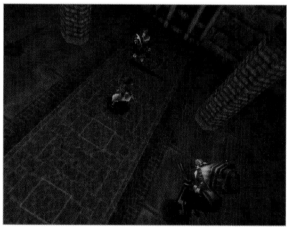

Eiji Aonuma, who today is the general producer for all things Zelda and has directed some of the series' best entries, got his start with the Zelda series by working on Ocarina of Time. He cites the game as his second-favorite Zelda game, saying it was his first opportunity to create a 3D world.

Along with the new perspective came dozens of new mechanics. Link was able to lock on to enemies while in combat. This is a feature that many 3D games would use following Ocarina of Time's release. Link could look around his world in first person and aim down the sights of items like the bow and arrow, hookshot, and slingshot.

This version of Hyrule had a day and night cycle with the sun on a constant rising and setting loop. The world changed during the night and changed the type of enemies Link would encounter.

Link also had a partner, Navi, who stays with him through the course of the game serving as your voice as well as your guide. This sort of character would become a regular part of future games—a companion that would help direct Link along his adventure.

Link to the Past established the idea of multiple worlds, but Ocarina took the idea in a new direction. At a certain point in the game, Link unlocked the ability to travel through time, allowing players to experience Link's life as a child, as well as an adult. It had a greater focus on non-player character interaction, and Link's ability to time travel meant you could meet characters as children, and return to them as adults to learn how they had changed or grown over that period of time.

Ocarina of Time also introduced Epona, Link's horse companion. Link could call on Epona at any time and ride her across the land of Hyrule for faster navigation and exploration.

However, there is one boy who does not have a fairy...

The Story

In Ocarina of Time, Link is a young orphan living with the Kokiri—a group of eternal children who each have a fairy as a companion. Link does not have a fairy, which has always made him an outsider in the small village.

The game opens with the Great Deku Tree sending a fairy to wake Link from a nightmare we later learn is about the evil Ganondorf stealing a young Princess Zelda. The Great Deku Tree knows of Link's important fate and sends him on a journey to recover the Master Sword and the Triforce. Link is successful, but Ganondorf steps in as Link is ready to take the Triforce, plunging the world into darkness and forcing Link to sleep for seven years.

Link wakes as an adult and discovers Ganondorf can be sent to the sacred realm, but only if he can gather the Seven Sages. A mysterious stranger appears named Sheik, who helps to guide him along his journey.

Link gathers the sages with the help of Sheik, who reveals her identity as Princess Zelda. As she reveals herself, however, Ganondorf steals her away and Link follows for the final confrontation.

The Items

The most important item Link discovers in Ocarina of Time is the Ocarina itself. It doesn't help him in combat, but Link can play the Ocarina to call his horse, solve puzzles, travel the world, and communicate with the many characters he meets.

Familiar Zelda items feel far different in the transition to 3D. Items like the bow and arrow, boomerang, and the hookshot

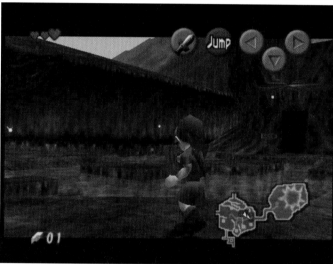

could be used from Link's point of view and the Lens of Truth allowed Link to literally look at invisible elements of the world.

Ocarina of Time also introduced the Bombchu, a special bomb that travels along the ground and walls. It allowed Link to send bombs to far away areas, or onto ceilings.

The Re-releases

Ocarina of Time has a strange history with re-releases. The game was originally released in 1998, and a follow-up version was planned that wasn't released as initially intended. A version of the game with rearranged dungeons was planned for a Nintendo 64 spinoff console called the 64DD, but it only came out in Japan and Nintendo abandoned it after it sold poorly.

This version of the game, however, did eventually come out in the form of the Master Quest on the GameCube. Nintendo offered this version of Ocarina of Time as a pre-order bonus for The Legend of Zelda: The Wind Waker. Ocarina of Time also appeared on a compilation disc included with certain special edition GameCubes. This disc included the original Zelda, Zelda II, and Majora's Mask, as well as Ocarina of Time.

In 2011, Ocarina of Time was completely remade for release on the Nintendo 3DS. This version of the game had improved visuals, stereoscopic 3D effects, and the option to play with motion controls, which allowed players to tilt the 3DS in order to aim items like the slingshot and bow and arrow, among others. This remade version of the game included the Master Quest, as well.

The Legend of Zelda: Ocarina of Time is also available on the Wii and Wii U Virtual Consoles.

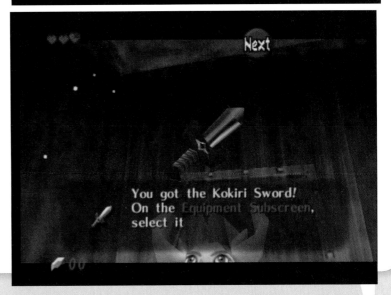

CHAPTER 8

The Legend of Zelda: Majora's Mask (Nintendo 64, 2000)

Ocarina of Time was a huge success for Nintendo. Majora's Mask was an attempt to build on that success by turning around a quick sequel. Majora's Mask was released two years after Ocarina of Time, a short amount of time considering it took four years of development before Ocarina of Time was released.

Majora's Mask was developer Eiji Aonuma's first chance to be in charge of a Zelda project. Today, Aonuma is the producer for the entire Zelda series and is generally considered to be in charge of the franchise.

The story in Majora's Mask is darker than the one in Ocarina. It takes place over a repeated three-day period as Link tries to stop the moon from crashing into the world. The game's cyclical nature, where players repeated the same three days over and over, was born from an idea from Nintendo developer Yoshiaki Koizumi. His idea involved a repeated cops-and-robbers scenario that was adapted for Zelda. It re-used many character models from Ocarina of Time, but makes it clear that while they might look the same, the characters are different from those you met in Ocarina of

Time. Seeing familiar characters in a new world gives the game a strange sense of dark mystery throughout.

Masks play an important part in the game. Link has his normal inventory of items, but also collects masks which help him solve puzzles, and transform. Alongside his normal child form, Link also uses masks to change into Deku, Goron, and Zora forms.

The Deku are a small plant-like enemy Link met in Ocarina of Time. The Goron are a race of rock creatures. The Zora are water creatures. When Link transforms, he is able to adopt their abilities. As a Deku, Link can fly in the air and shoot bubbles. As a Goron, he is powerful and can roll at fast speeds. As a Zora, Link can swim and breathe underwater.

The Story

Majora's Mask is a direct sequel to Ocarina of Time and starts with child Link and Epona on a journey to find Navi, his lost companion from Ocarina of Time. He is attacked by a scarecrow-like creature named Skull Kid, who Link met in Ocarina of Time.

Skull Kid is wearing a strange mask, and has two fairies with him. He steals Link's Ocarina and Epona and in the chase, Skull

Kid transforms Link into a Deku Scrub. This leads Link to the world of Termina and Clock Town, which is preparing for a Carnival of Time.

Link meets the Happy Mask Salesman (another character Link met in Ocarina, but only had a few minor interactions with) who tells him Skull Kid has stolen the dark and powerful Majora's Mask and as a result the moon is making its way toward Termina and will crash into the world in three days—unless Link can recover Majora's Mask and stop Skull Kid.

When Link recovers his Ocarina from Skull Kid, he learns he is able to go back in time three days to start his journey over, but he is able to keep the items and masks he has discovered to help him make more progress in his journey during each cycle.

During the three-day cycle, Link must deal with the people of Termina over the course of their three-day routines, and awaken four giants who are capable of stopping the moon's destructive course.

Majora's Mask is one of the few Zelda games that does not feature the Princess Zelda or Ganon. It also introduces the character Tingle. Tingle is a fairy-obsessed adult who refuses to grow up. He became a recurring character in Zelda after Majora's Mask, and even got his own spinoff in a

game called Freshly-Picked Tingle's Rosy Rupeeland for DS.

The Items

Majora's Mask does not feature many original items, as most of them appeared in Ocarina of Time. It does, however, include

24 masks with many in-game properties. A few of the masks allow Link to transform into completely different characters. Some masks provide bonuses, like the Bunny Ears, which allow Link to run faster. Some masks are purely for looks and are only used to start or complete certain side quests, like Kafei's Mask, which is used to learn about the character Kafei.

Collecting all the masks, which is not required in order to complete the game, unlocks the Fierce Deity Mask. The Fierce Deity Mask can be used during the final battle with Majora's Mask and transforms Link to his adult size and gives him a two-handed sword capable of firing lasers.

The Re-releases

Following its Nintendo 64 release, Majora's Mask appeared on a compilation disc for GameCube alongside the original Zelda, Zelda II, and Ocarina of Time. The disc came with certain special edition GameCube consoles. It was also released on the Wii and Wii U Virtual Consoles.

In 2015, the game was completely remade for 3DS. Much like the Ocarina of Time remake (which was handled by the same developer, Grezzo) Majora's Mask had updated visuals, stereoscopic 3D options, and motion control options. Unlike Ocarina of Time, however, Majora's Mask 3D featured some improvements. Time travel was handled differently, which led to less waiting around for certain events, and parts of the map were rearranged slightly to improve the flow of the game.

THE LEGEND OF ZELDA®
ORACLE OF
AGES™

PRESS START

© 2001 Nintendo

THE LEGEND OF ZELDA®
ORACLE OF
SEASONS™

PRESS START

© 2001 Nintendo

The Legend of Zelda: Oracle of Ages and Seasons (Game Boy Color, 2001)

Oracle of Ages and Seasons are two separate games that were released on two separate cartridges, but they came out at the same time and go together to make a complete Zelda experience.

The two games were the first Zelda titles not to be developed by Nintendo. Nintendo oversaw development closely, but the work was actually done by a studio called Flagship, which is part of Capcom. Capcom is known for the Street Fighter and Mega Man games. It was a surprise to see a studio other than Nintendo creating a Zelda title, but the

resulting games showed it was a bet that paid off.

The games actually started as part of a long-term plan for Flagship to create multiple Zelda games, starting with a Game Boy Color remake of the original Legend of Zelda for Game Boy. As development progressed, however, a number of technical challenges led to Flagship working on an original Zelda title.

The game plays and even looks like Link's Awakening. Art from that game, like Link's design, came over from his original Game

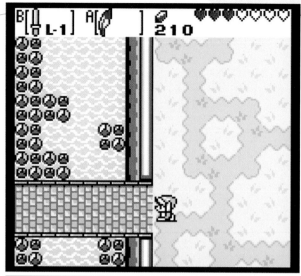

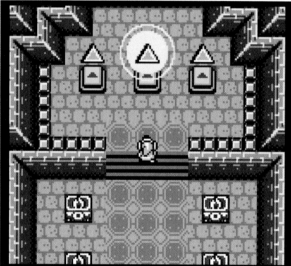

Boy release. It was the first original handheld Zelda game since Link's Awakening.

The games were first announced as three games: Mystical Seed of Power, Mystical Seed of Wisdom, and Mystical Seed of Courage. The plan was to allow players to start with any of the three games, but they gave up on that plan once they realized managing three games in this way would be too hard.

Oracle of Ages focuses on Zelda's puzzle solving and Oracle of Seasons focuses on Zelda's action. The two games have similar layouts, however, and offered passwords to use between the two games so the two could interact. The idea was you play through one game first, then play through the second, swapping passwords, and then unlock the game's true story and finale after beating both.

The two games were directed by Hidemaro Fujibayashi. Fujibayashi went on to direct more Zelda games after completing work on these two games, including handheld games Four Swords, The Minish Cap, and Phantom Hourglass. He also directed two console Zelda games, Skyward Sword and the most recent game in the series, Breath of the Wild.

The Story

The stories between Ages and Seasons is a complicated one that eventually connects, but each also works by itself.

In Ages, the Triforce calls out to Link, taking him to the land of Labrynna, where he finds Impa—Zelda's nursemaid—struggling against a dark force. Link saves her (just like he did in the original Zelda) and together they find Nayru, who is the Oracle of Ages. She is possessed by the evil Veran, Sorceress

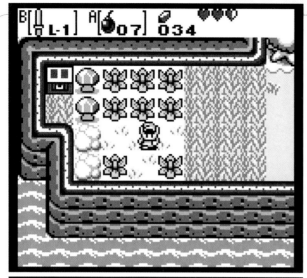

of Shadows, and Link must find the eight Essences of Time in order to save her.

Oracle of Seasons follows a similar story. The Triforce calls out to Link, bringing him to the world of Holodrum, where he meets Din, the Oracle of Seasons, and her attendant, Impa. Onox, General of Darkness, steals Din away and Link learns he must collect the eight Essences of Nature in order to defeat Onox.

And just as he celebrated at the end of Ages, Twinrova appears to light the Flame of Destruction, which brings you to the game's true final battle.

The Items

There are many different items between the two games, but there are a number that appear in both, as well. Some items came

straight from Ocarina of Time, like the Bombchu and the Biggoron sword.

The hookshot only appears in Ages, and Roc's Feather (and later cape) only appear in Seasons. Oracle of Ages also features the Harp of Ages, which allows Link to control time, while Seasons features the Rod of Seasons, which allows Link to control seasons.

When played on a Game Boy Advance system, players could also access the Advance Shop. In the shop, a character named Stockwell will sell you a pair of magic rings and a Gasha seed for 100 rupees each.

Both games also have a focus on collecting seeds for various missions and puzzles.

The Re-releases

The two games were released at the same time in 2001, right before the launch of the Game Boy Advance. In 2013, both games were released for the 3DS Virtual Console.

CHAPTER 10

The Legend of Zelda: Four Swords

(Game Boy Advance, 2002)

Bundled with the 2002 re-release of A Link to the Past for Game Boy Advance, Four Swords marks Zelda's first experimentation with multiplayer, featured its own canonical story, and was later sold separately as a downloadable title on the DSi and 3DS eShop. These factors together are enough to make it stand alone as its own Zelda entry and it is not considered a spinoff.

Upon its initial release, the game could only be played in multiplayer. The game would be re-released later with a mode allowing players to play by themselves. Development of Minish Cap (which would release two years later) was paused so the team could work on the Link to the Past port and complete development on Four Swords. It uses Minish Cap's art style, and also introduced players to Vaati, who would be the main villain in both Minish Cap and Four Swords Adventures.

The game scales depending on how many are playing, between two and four, and uses randomized levels to encourage replayability. Two or more players would work their way through a randomized level and meet a boss at the end. The quicker players defeated the boss, the more rupees

they would get, which are needed in order to confront Vaati. It's a short game and is less reliant on puzzles for progression.

approach and Vaati appears, stealing Zelda away. Link grabs the Four Sword, is broken into multiple Links, and leaves to confront Vaati.

The Story

Four Swords features one of Zelda's simplest stories. Link and Zelda check on the Four Sword to make sure it is continuing to seal the evil sorcerer Vaati. It breaks on their

The Items

Unlike most Zelda games, Link can hold only hold one item at a time in Four Swords and they are usually intended to be used in a specific level. There are plenty of common items like the bow and arrow, bombs, or a shield, but it does have a few game-specific items. The Magnetic Gloves, for example, only appear in Oracle of Seasons and Four Swords, and let Link move items remotely. The Gnat hat appears exclusively in Four Swords. It allows Link to shrink in size, something he would do again two years later in Minish Cap, but this is the only time that ability is tied to a specific item.

The Re-release

After its release as a bonus game in the Game Boy Advance re-release of Link to the Past, Four Swords received two additional re-releases with some updates. In 2011 Four Swords: Anniversary Edition released as a downloadable DSiWare game for the DSi and was later made available on 3DS eShop. The Anniversary Edition of the game added a single-player mode as well as two new stages, the Realm of Memories and Hero's Trial.

CHAPTER 11

The Legend of Zelda: The Wind Waker (GameCube, 2003)

The Wind Waker was Zelda's first game on the GameCube. The look of Wind Waker was much different than earlier games, and many fans didn't like it and felt it was too cartoony. That opinion, however, has changed over time.

Part of the reason fans didn't like the style of Wind Waker was because how different it was from the previous console Zelda games, Ocarina of Time and Majora's Mask. Both of those games took a darker, more mature direction for the Legend of Zelda. Expectations for a more realistic Zelda were also set by a brief clip shown at the 2000 Nintendo Space World trade show. The video showed Ocarina of Time's Link and Ganon rendered with the recently revealed GameCube's graphical capabilities. A Zelda game with that visual style was never in development. The video was made to show off what the GameCube was capable, not what Nintendo was working on. When Wind Waker looked like a cartoon it was a surprise and many thought the serious themes from Ocarina and Majora's Mask had simply been replaced by bright colors and goofy faces. That was not the case.

Aside from the change in style, Wind Waker made another massive change to Zelda in that it removed the ground. Wind Waker takes place in a version of Hyrule covered in water, referred to as the Great Sea in the game, with small islands dotting the landscape. Link travels by boat and lives life like a pirate, visiting the world's many islands to complete dungeons, solve puzzles, defeat monsters, and save the day.

The game was a huge step forward in terms of Link's facial expressions. In Link's previous 3D adventures, his face and general movement were limited by technology. But here, with the GameCube's animation capabilities, you knew exactly what he was thinking without him saying a word. Link's eyes grew when he was scared, he laughed when he was happy, and showed anger and determination when it was time to fight.

The Story

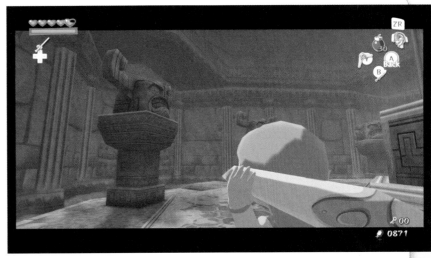

Wind Waker begins with a young Link living a normal life with his sister, Aryll, and grandmother on Outset Island, a small island with a small community.

The island has a tradition of dressing its young men in green tunics in order to honor their coming of age, as well as the legendary Hero of Time. As Link is preparing his celebrations, a giant bird drops a young woman on their island, and Link makes an effort to find and save her. He is successful and meets Tetra, the pirate captain.

The bird changes his focus to Aryll, and steals her away. Tetra informs Link that this bird is stealing young girls with long ears, and agrees to take him to

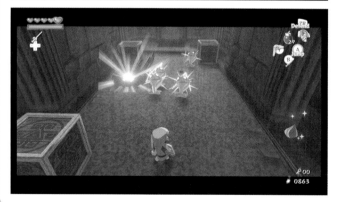

the Forsaken Fortress so he may attempt to save her.

He is unsuccessful, but he meets a talking boat named The King of Red Lions that tells Link the bird that stole his sister belongs to Ganon, who is seeking Zelda's heir. Link must find the three Pearls of the Goddesses in order to discover the Hero of Time's power.

When Link gathers the pearls, The King of Red Lions takes him underwater to a Hyrule suspended in time, where he is able to retrieve the Master Sword. It's not enough, however, and Link is defeated by Ganon, who has found Zelda's heir, Tetra.

Ganon steals Tetra away, and Link attempts to gather the eight scattered shards of the Triforce of Courage.

Link meets Ganon again in the underwater Hyrule, and he and Tetra (Zelda) work together in an attempt to defeat him.

The Items

The Wind Waker is an item in the game. It is a conductor's baton that Link is able to use to direct the wind to serve his needs when traveling. Other items that don't appear in other games, or appeared in Wind Waker

first, include the Grappling Hook and Deku Leaf.

The Grappling Hook can be used as a weapon, but also allows Link to swing between ledges, or pull certain items toward him. The Deku Leaf has so far only appeared in Wind Waker, but it has appeared in other forms in follow-up Zelda games. Link uses the leaf as a fan to create wind and can also hold it above his head and use it like a parachute when jumping from large heights.

Other items include the classics, like the hook shot, bow and arrow, and Picto Box.

The Re-release

Despite a number of popular GameCube games receiving Wii ports to take advantage of its new motion-control capabilities, Wind Waker did not re-emerge until 2013 when The Wind Waker HD was re-released on Wii U.

The game received a new look for its Wii U debut, with

improved lighting and color throughout. The re-release also improved the sailing gameplay by allowing players to unlock the Swift Sail, which let players move through the water faster without the need to stop the boat in order to change direction. It also improved the pacing of the game's final quest—tracking the scattered pieces of the Triforce of Courage.

Wind Waker HD also allows Link to turn the Picto Box camera toward himself in order to take selfies.

CHAPTER 12

The Legend of Zelda: Four Swords Aventures (GameCube, 2004)

Four Swords Adventures (not to be confused with the handheld game, Four Swords) was released about a year after Wind Waker and took the usual single-player experience in a multiplayer direction. The game can be played alone, but it was designed with four players in mind. Its focus is more on action than puzzle and story, but Four Swords Adventures does include those things too.

Four Swords Adventures is probably the most difficult Zelda game to play. It's not because it's harder than other Zelda games—it has to do with the number of people and consoles you need. To play

with two or more players, each must have a Game Boy Advance handheld console and a GameCube to Game Boy Advance Link cable.

Each player controls a Link, one colored the traditional green, the others colored purple, blue, or red, as they make their way through a series of challenges. With the aid of the Game Boy Advance, players can split up to enter caves and houses separate from the group, at which time the action will shift to that player's Game Boy Advance screen. In this way, Four Swords Adventures

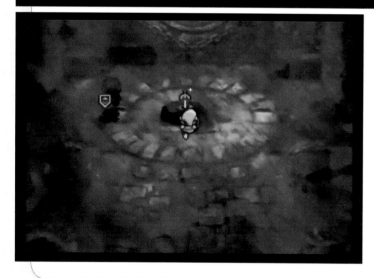

paved the way for the Wii U's two-screen mechanics.

Visually, the game borrows from A Link to the Past and Wind Waker. Link's design is a 2D version of Wind Waker Link, named Toon Link, and the environments and gameplay are modeled after Link to the Past. The music also features different versions of Link to the Past's music.

Unlike traditional Zelda titles, which take place in large open worlds, Four Swords Adventures takes place over a series of levels.

The Story

Zelda gathers herself and the maiden descendants of the Seven Sages to help strengthen what she suspects to be the weakened seal currently containing the evil Sorcerer of Winds, Vaati. She brings Link along with her for protection, and when she and the maidens attempt to strengthen the seal, a dark version of Link appears and steals away the maidens and Zelda.

Link follows this shadowy version of himself and is led to the Four Sword, which is stuck in a pedestal. Link pulls the sword out and it splits him into the four Links. He also accidentally broke the seal containing Vaati.

Vaati's release plunges the world into darkness, and opens a portal to the Dark World, releasing evil twins of the Knights of Hyrule. The four Links work together to defeat

the evil Knights of Hyrule and learn that Ganon orchestrated Vaati's release and the creation of the dark Link in order to build his evil army and gather as much evil energy as possible.

The Links must then work together to retrieve each of the kidnapped maidens.

The Items

Unlike other Zelda games, only a few of the items discovered in Four Swords stay in your inventory. For example, you might find the boomerang in one level, but Link is unable to use it in the next, unless he can find it again. They're treated like temporary power-ups more than true items.

Almost all the items are borrowed from Link to the Past, as that is the game Four Swords is most similar to. Some interesting but non-exclusive items include Force Gems and Roc's Feather. Force Gems are needed to complete each level. Roc's Feather is an interesting addition here, because although it had appeared in previous Zelda games, this is the first time it appeared in a console Zelda game.

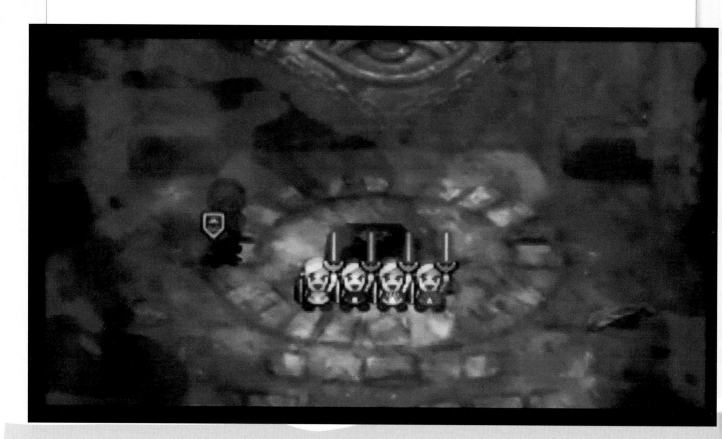

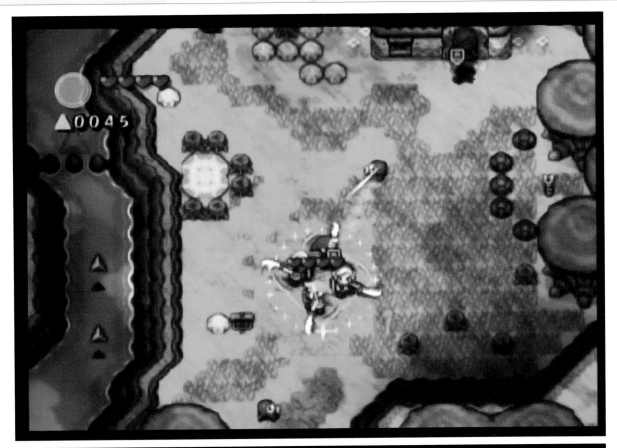

CHAPTER 13

The Legend of Zelda: The Minish Cap

(Game Boy Advance, 2005)

After its success with Oracle of Ages and Seasons, Capcom returned for another handheld Zelda game. But unlike the Oracle games, Minish Cap was a much more straightforward Zelda game. One release. One story. One game.

Minish Cap, the Link to the Past Game Boy Advance version, and the Oracle games are the only original core Zelda games to be created outside of Nintendo. Minish Cap was produced by Keiji Inafune, who helped create Mega Man and worked closely on many other well-known Capcom games.

The game follows the pattern established by Link to the Past, taking place from an overhead perspective. It uses the art style established in the Four Swords game with its general art direction following Wind Waker. The game also dives deeper into the characters from the Four Swords games, expanding the story of those games, as well as the wider story of the expanded Zelda universe.

The Minish, which Hyrule citizens call the Picori, are a race of tiny creatures that can only be seen by children. They play a crucial role in the game's story and are credited

with creating the Four Sword. During the game, Link earns the ability to shrink down to the size of the Minish in order to communicate with them, solve puzzles, and explore areas of the game from a whole new perspective.

Alongside the usual Zelda gameplay, Minish Cap also expanded Link's combat abilities. Outside of his standard sword-swipe and item-specific abilities, Link could use Tiger Scrolls to learn better moves, like being able to perform a powerful attack with your sword after completing a roll.

The game also introduced the Kinstone system, which rewarded you for interacting with every non-player character in the game. Matching your Kinstone with other characters opened up secrets in the world.

Curiously, Minish Cap was released after the launch of the DS. The first model of DS was able to play Game Boy advance games, but the game did not feature any additional features by being played on Nintendo's new console.

The Story

Link and Zelda are childhood friends in Minish Cap's opening, preparing to visit the Picori Festival together. As the legend goes (a different legend than the Zelda one on this particular occasion), the world was filled with darkness and monsters until the Picori gifted the Hero of Man the Picori Blade, which used the magic of light to banish the darkness. A festival is held every year to honor the Picori and their blade.

The evil Vaati enters the festival's sword tournament and wins the right to touch the Picori Blade. He breaks the sword and lets monsters loose on the world, and turns Princess Zelda into stone. The only way to change things back to normal is to find the Picori and have them restore the blade, and since the Picori only reveal themselves to children, Link takes on the challenge.

On his way to the Minish Woods to try and find the Picori, Link finds a talking hat named Ezlo who also doesn't like Vaati (because he turned him into a hat). The two

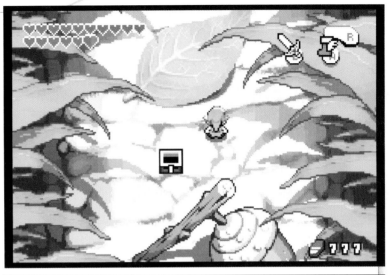

team up, find the Minish, and learn that Link must recover the four elemental objects in order to repair the Picori Blade.

During the course of the adventure, Link learns Ezlo's relationship is much deeper than simply being annoyed with the wizard for turning him into a hat. Ezlo is a sorcerer himself and Vaati was his apprentice, before he went mad with power and decided to lash out at the world of man.

The Items

Minish Cap has a handful of new items, as well as different versions of previous items, alongside the collection of standards like the bomb, bow and arrow, and bottles.

The Gust Jar inhales air and other items, and can also spit out large gusts of winds. Link uses it to blow things out of his way, but also uses it for navigation. When standing on

mobile platforms, Link can use the Gust Jar to push himself in certain directions.

The mole mitts essentially replace the shovel, which has appeared in many Zelda games, and allows Link to dig at high speeds.

Minish Cap also introduced the Cane of Pacci, which can create trampolines in shallow holes, and can also flip over any object.

The Re-releases

There are two ways to play Minish Cap on modern consoles. The first, and easiest, is on the Wii U. The game is available on the console's Virtual Console. The game is also available on the 3DS, but is only available to 3DS users who purchased the handheld within the first few months of its release.

Shortly after the launch of the 3DS, Nintendo cut the handheld's price by $80, and in an effort to reward those 3DS players who had paid full price, they were given a handful of free downloadable games and one of them was Minish Cap. Since then, Nintendo has released a number of Game Boy and Game Boy Color games on the 3DS Virtual Console, but not Game Boy Advance, which means the only way to get Minish Cap on your 3DS is to already have it.

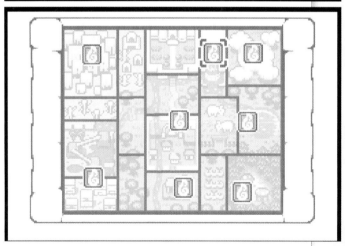

CHAPTER 14

The Legend of Zelda: Twilight Princess (Wii, 2006)

Despite the popularity of Wind Waker, fans still missed the darker tone and more realistic visual direction of some of Zelda's earlier games. When Twilight Princess was revealed, fans were thrilled. It showed an adult Link in a much more realistic art style, and the return of Epona. The world looked darker, the enemies scarier, and Link could battle on horseback. There were rumors that grown men cried at the press conference where the game's first footage was shown.

Supposedly, the game's main idea—being able to switch between human and wolf form—was the product of a dream from Eiji Aonuma. Aonuma lists Twilight Princess as his third-favorite Zelda game, saying he set out to make a better game than Ocarina of Time, which is considered by many to be the best of the series.

Announced as a GameCube title, Twilight Princess was delayed several times leading up to its release as a result of the decision to switch the game over to Nintendo's new platform, the Wii. The majority of the game's development time was spent building a game that used standard controls, so adding motion controls proved to be a lot of work, especially considering many developers

were unsure how to use Nintendo's new controller.

The game did finally come out, however, as a Wii launch title, with a GameCube version of the game releasing about a month later. For many, the game served as an introduction point to motion controls and it helped boost the Wii to become the huge success that it became. It's not often a Nintendo platform launches with a brand-new Zelda game. It wouldn't happen again until the launch of the Nintendo Switch and Breath of the Wild in 2017.

Since the beginning, Link has held his sword in his left hand, but since players using the Wii's motion controls, regardless of hand preference, held and swung the Wii Remote in their right hand, Link reflected that by being right-handed for the first time. The GameCube version, however, kept Link's true hand preference.

The Story

Link begins the game as a farmer in Ordon Village. The town's children are kidnapped and Link gets pulled into the Twilight Realm and transformed into a wolf while attempting to save the children.

In his new wolf form, Link meets Midna, a mysterious twilight creature who is willing to help him as long as he helps her. She directs Wolf Link to Zelda, who explains she was forced to surrender Hyrule to Zant, the King of the Twilight. Link learns he must revive the Light Spirits to save Hyrule, and Midna offers to help knowing she will be able to acquire Fused Shadows along the way.

After reviving the Light Spirts, saving Ordon's children, and tracking down Midna's Fused Shadows, Link learns that Midna and Zant are from the same tribe, but have different goals. Zelda sacrifices herself to save Midna, making her find new respect for Link's

world of light, and helping her decide to truly help Link.

Link tracks down the Master Sword and the duo discovers Zant attempted to shatter the Mirror of Twilight, which is the only entrance to the Twilight Realm. Link and Midna track down the pieces of the mirror, confront Zant, and learn that he struck a deal with Ganondorf and that Midna is the true ruler of the Twilight Realm.

The Items

Nintendo took full advantage of the Wii's motion controls by using pointer controls for the items Link aims, like his bow and arrow, slingshot, and hookshot (known as the clawshot in Twilight Princess). The fishing rod also benefitted from the added motion controller, but the game has plenty of other items that were not dependent on the Wii's new control scheme.

The ball and chain is a giant heavy ball attached to a chain. It's an item Link can throw like a wrecking ball.

The Spinner is the rare Zelda item that only appeared in a single Zelda game (to date). It's a spinning cog that Link can stand on top of and use to move quickly, or in some specific cases, climb walls.

The Dominion Rod allows Link to bring statues to life and control them remotely.

Familiar items also received interesting twists. The boomerang, renamed the Gale Boomerang, throws out mini tornadoes when thrown. The clawshot could be upgraded to a double clawshot, allowing Link to pull himself toward multiple walls without ever having to place his feet on the ground.

The Re-releases

Twilight Princess' first releases followed a strange path. The Wii version of the game came out first, followed by the GameCube version about a month later. The GameCube version of the game is a mirrored version of the Wii game in order to compensate for Link being left-handed. Rather than change Link's animations or rework his design to function as a right-handed character, Nintendo flipped the whole game.

Another small change between the Wii version and the GameCube version? The Wii version is playable in widescreen. The GameCube version can only be played in fullscreen resolution.

In 2016, Twilight Princess received a high-definition overhaul for Wii U. The visuals were improved, though not to the same degree as the Wind Waker HD Wii U port. The GameCube version of the game is the one that received the upgrade, so it finally allowed players to use the left-handed Link in widescreen. It also added amiibo functionality, where Nintendo's Zelda figures could unlock bonuses like extra hearts or inventory items. Finally, a new challenge area for Wolf Link was added that could only be accessed by players who have the Wolf Link amiibo—a figure that was included with the game. That amiibo could also be used to summon Wolf Link as a companion in Breath of the Wild.

CHAPTER 15

The Legend of Zelda: Phantom Hourglass (DS, 2007)

Minish Cap was released a few months after the launch of the Nintendo DS. You could play it on the handheld thanks to its backward compatibility, but Phantom Hourglass was the first true Zelda game for the two-screened system.

Phantom Hourglass is a direct sequel to The Wind Waker, picking up right where the GameCube game left off. Toon Link returns, as well as Tetra and her Zelda identity, continuing their adventures on an ocean-covered version of Hyrule.

Eiji Aonuma cites Phantom Hourglass as his personal favorite Zelda game. It was Aonuma's first time in the producer role after directing the previous few Zelda games.

The game took full advantage of the Nintendo DS' additional touchscreen, serving as a showcase of the kind of games the DS could deliver. The game used buttons only here and there, and Link was controlled entirely with the touchscreen. Link would follow the stylus wherever you pressed it to the screen, and a quick slash on the touchscreen would make Link perform a sword slash.

You could also use the touchscreen to draw a path for your boat and take notes

on the map. You could blow into the DS' microphone to create wind, and for one puzzle you actually had to close the DS in order to copy something from the top screen to the bottom screen. It also had a limited multiplayer mode that players could play online against other players. It was not the first Zelda multiplayer game (that was Four Swords), but it was the first Zelda game to offer an online multiplayer option.

102

As part of the game's ongoing story, Link had to revisit the Temple of the Ocean King. This area plays out like a large dungeon, but Link is only able to stay in the dungeon for so long, and must return to it throughout the game.

The Story

At the end of Wind Waker, Ganon had been turned to stone and dropped to the bottom of the sea. As one might expect, statues stuck on the ocean floor are not a threat. Ganon does not appear in Phantom Hourglass, but that doesn't mean that Link is completely in the clear.

The game starts with Link and Tetra (Princess Zelda's heir) exploring the ocean and coming across a ghost ship. The two board the ship and run into trouble when Zelda

is turned into stone and stolen away as Link falls into the ocean.

He wakes up on the shore of an island where a fairy named Ciela and an old man named Oshus catch Link up on what happened on the ghost ship and how to save Princess Zelda. Link contracts the boat captain, Linebeck, to help him on his journey. Captain Linebeck only agrees to help after receiving promises of treasure, and even then continues to whine through the course of the game.

Link learns Ceila and Oshus are magical beings hiding from Bellum, the monster that created the ghost ship and turned Zelda into stone. To defeat Bellum, Link has to craft the Phantom Sword and take it to the Temple of the Ocean King for the final battle.

During the final battle, Captain Linebeck makes up for all of his complaining by helping to hold off Bellum when Link gets knocked out temporarily.

Hah! Some legendary hero

The Items

Many of Link's items from Wind Waker appear in Phantom Hourglass. Link gets his Grappling Hook back, for example, an item that only appears in those two games.

Other old items have new uses in the Phantom Hourglass, thanks to the touchscreen gameplay. The path of both the Boomerang and Bomchu can be traced on screen for more accuracy.

The Phantom Hourglass is also an item. It serves as a timer for when Link enters the Temple of the Ocean King. Link can only stay in the temple for a certain amount of time, which is dictated by the Phantom Hourglass and how much Sand of Hours Link is able to put into it.

The Re-releases

There are two ways to play Phantom Hourglass on modern Nintendo consoles. The original game is compatible with the 3DS, meaning the cartridge will work on Nintendo's latest handheld.

The game has also been released on the Wii U Virtual Console, which is the first time the game could be played on a television screen.

CHAPTER 16

The Legend of Zelda: Spirit Tracks (DS, 2009)

Zelda's second release for DS borrowed nearly all the gameplay from Phantom Hourglass. The setting, however, offered a big change. It still used Wind Waker's art direction with cartoon visuals, but Link was no longer on the ocean. Now he was on land and controlling a train.

The Zelda games have always taken place in a medieval land, but Spirit Tracks saw Link taking a technological leap forward and introduced the industrial revolution. He still used a sword and shield to keep enemies at bay, but now Link was using a train to explore his world.

The touchscreen still acts as the game's main interface with players controlling Link by using the lower screen to direct Link and his combat. When on the train, players used the touchscreen to map out a path and pull on the train's whistle to alert animals to get off the track.

The game continued to allow players to make notes on the map and blow on the microphone for certain parts of the game. Link's instrument in Spirit Tracks is a pan flute, and players had to blow into the microphone in order to play it.

Spirit Tracks also has the Tower of Spirits, a large dungeon that Link must return to throughout the game making a little progress each time he visits. Unlike Phantom Hourglass' similar Temple of the Ocean King, progress in the Tower of Spirits is based on making it to certain checkpoints, and not a timer.

Spirit Tracks casts Zelda in a new role for the first time. She's not the damsel in distress in Spirit Tracks. She still needs Link's help, but she joins you for the whole journey as a spirit. She offers tips and plays an important part in your progress. She can also possess the Phantom Guardians, the enemies from Phantom Hourglass that impeded your progress in the Temple of the Ocean King.

The Story

Link is a young train conductor at the opening of Spirit Tracks. He is preparing to travel to Hyrule Castle in order to receive his engineer's certificate from Princess Zelda. While there, Zelda secretly asks Link to meet her later as she doesn't trust her advisor, Chancellor Cole.

Hyrule's train tracks are disappearing. No one knows why, but Zelda suspects it may have to do with something happening at the nearby Tower of Spirits. She asks Link, an official engineer, to take her there. As they are traveling to the tower, the tracks disappear, causing the train to crash as the Tower of Spirits breaks apart into pieces off in the distance.

Chancellor Cole reveals himself as a horned demon (something he hid by wearing two hats) and uses magic to separate Zelda's spirit from her body.

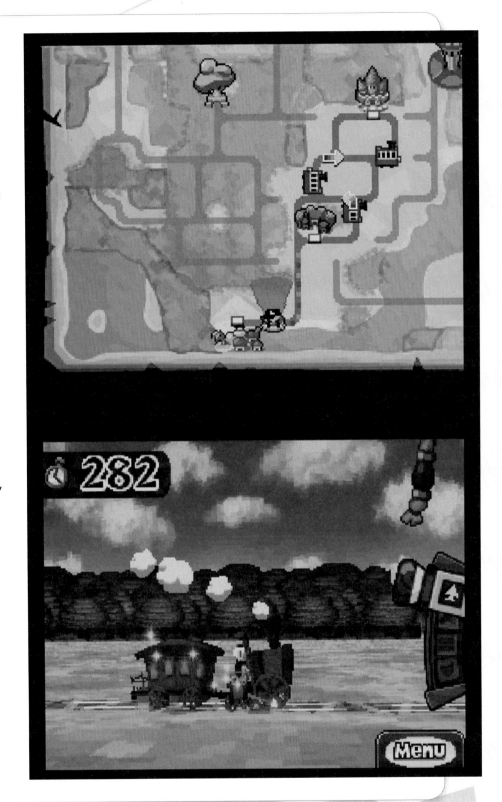

The Tower of Spirits and the train tracks leading to it, called the Spirit Tracks, were built to imprison the Demon King Malladus, a villain Chancellor Cole seeks to release onto Hyrule. Despite restoring the Spirit Tracks, Malladus uses Zelda's body as a way to resurrect himself, and he and Cole enter the Dark Realm.

Zelda and Link follow after acquiring the Compass of Light and Bow of Light, leading to the final fight.

The Items

Spirit Tracks features three original items, two of which would appear in later Zelda games. The Whirlwind is a take on items like the Gust Jar and Deku Leaf, which allow you to manipulate wind, but it's also like the boomerang, in that you can use it to pull items toward you.

The Whip does not have a creative name, but it has some creative uses. It works a little like the grappling hook and can also stun enemies.

The Sand Rod allows Link to create blocks of sand, either as a way to block a path or raise something into the air. Link can also stand on his blocks of sand to solve certain puzzles.

The Re-releases

There are two ways to play Spirit Tracks on modern Nintendo consoles. The original game is compatible with the 3DS, meaning the cartridge will work on Nintendo's latest handheld.

The game has also been released on the Wii U Virtual Console, marking the first time the game can be played on a television screen.

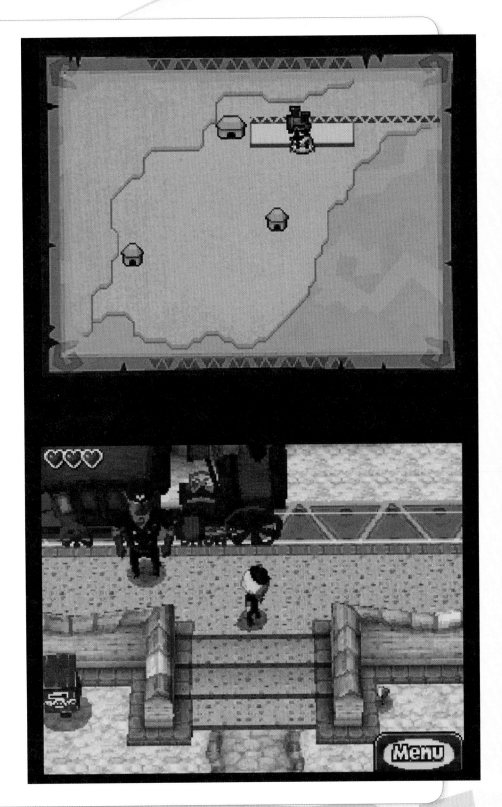

A Examine

CHAPTER 17

The Legend of Zelda: Skyward Sword (Wii, 2011)

There were a number of handheld Zelda games released after Twilight Princess in 2006, but it wasn't until 2011 that another console Zelda game was released. Skyward Sword was the first true Wii exclusive Zelda game. Where Twilight Princess was technically an upgraded port of a GameCube game, Skyward Sword was developed from the beginning to be a Wii game.

The game required the use of the Wii MotionPlus controller, which was an enhanced version of the Wii Remote, offering better motion tracking and a number of other improved features to the original Wii Remote. Where Twilight Princess sensed movement in the controller and played the sword swinging animation in response, Skyward Sword offered true one-to-one movement. Raise the controller slowly over your head, and Link would do the same. Hold up the sword to block an incoming attack, and Link would do the same.

Skyward Sword had some problems, but the technology worked exactly as Nintendo intended. The game was released five years into the Wii's lifespan, but in many ways it was one of the first games to deliver the kind

of gameplay experience the Wii had always promised.

Skyward Sword took Link's adventure to the sky, exchanging his horse for a giant bird that could fly. Link's home is in the clouds, as was much of its gameplay. Link explored the air visiting floating islands to complete tasks and parachuted his way to the land below in order to do battle with the evil that resided there. The game also gave Zelda a more important part and established some important story details for Zelda's wider universe.

Before the game was even released, Nintendo confirmed that Skyward Sword was the very first Zelda story on the larger timeline.

Skyward Sword's music is notable as it was the first in the series to be recorded by an orchestra. Past games had used digitized music for their soundtracks. The live orchestra gave the game's soundtrack a larger, soaring feeling. Special editions of the game included the soundtrack as a bonus.

The Story

Skyward Sword begins with teenage Link completing his knight training in the world of Skyloft. He is childhood friends with Zelda and is in constant competition with Groose, a local bully who is frustrated by Zelda's lack of interest in him. Zelda's characterization is notable in this game, as she is a far more realized character than she is previous Zelda games. She is also not a princess. She is the daughter of Gaepora, the headmaster of the knight academy. Skyward Sword's writers wanted players to have more incentive for saving Zelda outside of just her being a princess in danger.

While celebrating graduation by flying their birds around Skyloft, Zelda is pulled out of the sky by a dark tornado and Link is injured. While recovering back home, Link is called to retrieve the Goddess Sword, which is protected in a large statue located in his Skyloft home.

The voice calling him is Fi, the spirit of the Goddess Sword, who tells Link about the Demon King Demise, who had destroyed

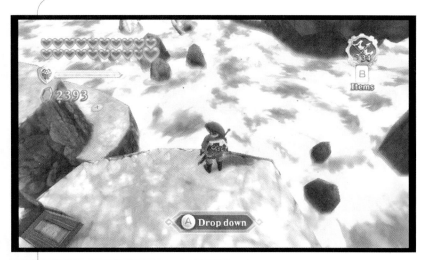

the land below in his attempts to acquire the Triforce.

Zelda is on her own unseen adventure, and Link must track her down by exploring the world's surface. He meets Impa, a woman tasked with protecting Zelda, and Ghirahim, the mysterious sorcerer who is working toward bringing Demise back to life.

Link's adventure takes him back and forth through time where he must fight the Imprisoned, a giant beast attempting to break the seal holding back Demise. Link fights the beast multiple times and is able to hold him back with Groose's help, but realizes he must power up the Goddess Sword by completing a series of trials so he can finally defeat Demise.

Zelda crystalizes herself into a seal to help hold back Demise. Link finally finds the Triforce and frees Zelda. Ghirahim appears, however, steals Zelda, and goes back in time to an era where Demise has not yet been eliminated.

Link follows Ghirahim back in time with his newly powered-up sword (which is now the Master

Sword). Link and Demise do battle and the villain curses Link and Zelda's bloodlines to forever be forced to fight against evil.

The Items

Skyward Sword's items take the usual Zelda items and add some motion control twists to them. When you pretend to shoot an arrow from a bow with the Wii Remote Nunchuck, Link does the same thing. You can also catch bugs by swinging around a bug net as you would in the real world.

The Beetle is one of Skyward Sword's few new items. It's a remote control flying beetle that Link can use to retrieve items or activate faraway switches.

The whip item, which appeared in Spirit Tracks, also works well with the Wii Remote's motion functionality.

It's not a motion controlled item, but Link's Sail Cloth, given to him by Zelda at the beginning of the game, allows him to avoid fall damage.

Almost all the items could also be upgraded to stronger versions.

The Re-release

Skyward Sword is compatible with the Wii U thanks to backward compatibility, and the game was also made available to download from the Wii U's online store. That version of the game, however, is a direct port of the Wii game with no improvements in place to take advantage of the Wii U's superior graphics.

CHAPTER 18

The Legend of Zelda: A Link Between Worlds (3DS, 2013)

Even though many fans liked the touchscreen gameplay of Phantom Hourglass and Spirit Tracks, Zelda's first 3DS game went back to using standard controls. It did offer something new, however, in a number of ways related the structure of the game and how the player pursues its challenges.

A Link Between Worlds is a successor of sorts to Link to the Past for the Super Nintendo. In Japan, Link Between Worlds' title translates roughly to Triforce of the Gods 2. Triforce of the Gods was Link to the Past's Japanese subtitle. The game uses the basic Hyrule layout of Link to the Past and features a similar art direction, but feels very different.

The game's biggest new feature is how players make progress. Instead of working through each dungeon in a specific order according to the game's storyline, players were free to tackle any dungeon in any order they chose. Items could be rented from a local salesman and taken to your dungeon of choice. Eventually, the items can be bought and owned, but for the purposes of pursuing any puzzle you want, every item is available right from the start. Years prior, Zelda producer Eiji Aonuma stated

THE LEGEND OF

ZELDA™

A LINK BETWEEN WORLDS

© 2013 Nintendo

he wanted to mix up Zelda's structure and make it feel fresh by opening the game up to more player-driven direction. Letting players tackle dungeons in any order they chose was one of the first examples of Aonuma trying new things with Zelda.

Early in the game, Link also unlocks the ability to turn into a painting and flatten himself against walls. This is used to solve puzzles, avoid enemies, and travel to an alternate version of Hyrule called Lorule.

Lorule is similar to Link to the Past's Dark World, but acts more like a reverse

Hyrule with different versions of characters you meet in the normal Hyrule, including versions of Zelda and Ganondorf.

The Story

A Link Between Worlds takes place many centuries after the events of Link to the Past on Super Nintendo. Link works for a blacksmith. He is delivering a sword to Hyrule castle when he meets Yuga, a sorceress who knocks Link out.

Link is woken up by Ravio, a merchant in a purple robe wearing a bunny mask. He gives Link a bracelet and Link goes to tell Princess Zelda what has happened. She sends him on a mission to track down the Master Sword, and he returns with it just in time to see Zelda being turned into a painting by Yuga.

Link chases her through a portal and ends up in Lorule, a dark and twisted version of Hyrule. There he meets Hilda, Zelda's counterpart. Eventually, Link, Hilda, Zelda, and Ravio must work together to help restore Lorule's Triforce and bring light back to Hilda's kingdom.

Ravio

Welcome back, Mr. Hero!

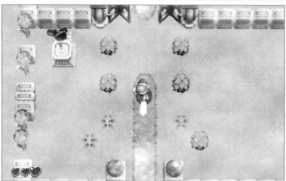

The Items

A Link Between Worlds features no truly original items, but it does feature some rare ones. The Sand Rod, which first appeared in Spirit Tracks, appears here with similar functions. Link uses it to craft blocks of sand, which he can use as a bridge, or to raise objects into the air.

The Tornado Rod is another wind item that creates a small tornado. It can lift Link in the air, as well as objects on the ground.

At the start of the game, every item can be rented from Ravio, and they function the

same as they do when you are able to purchase them later in the game, but Ravio's rentable ones have little purple bunny ears on them identifying them as being rented.

All of Link's items can be upgraded to improved forms by collecting the missing babies of a Mother Maiamai. Every 10 babies you bring her rewards Link with an upgraded version of your items.

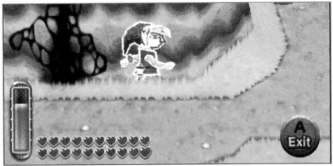

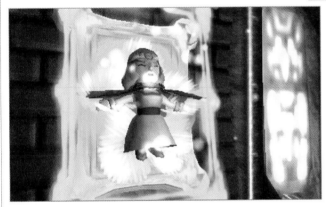

Painting IV: The Hero Awakens

CHAPTER 19

The Legend of Zelda: Tri Force Heroes (3DS, 2015)

Tri Force Heroes is a direct sequel to Link Between Worlds. It features the same Link as he continues his journey and uses the same visuals and general gameplay. However, Tri Force Heroes has a lot more in common with the Four Swords games.

Tri Force is not an open-world Zelda, and instead plays out over a series of levels. The levels are designed for three players to play together, though a single player controlling three Links can make it through the game successfully.

The main goal of the game isn't to collect new items or solve puzzles, but rather to collect clothes with special abilities. Link can put together costumes by beating or replaying the same levels. Along with the customization options that go alongside unlocking the costumes, they each offer specific bonuses. Some outfits might offer more health, or make you fire off three arrows instead of just one.

Combat works like it did in Link Between Worlds. Players don't collect permanent items, but instead grab temporary items like bows and arrows and boomerangs to use in single levels. Many of the game's puzzles and battles require the three Links to stand

THE LEGEND OF
ZELDA™
Tri Force Heroes

©2015 Nintendo
Codeveloped by GREZZO

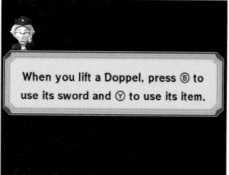

When you lift a Doppel, press Ⓑ to use its sword and Ⓨ to use its item.

Deku Forest - 1 -

🧚 × 3

Loading...

on each other's shoulders to form a stack of Links.

The game offers local and online multiplayer options, and also offered free downloadable content after the game launched that expanded the game's world. Strangely, the game can only be played by a three-player team, or a single player. There is no option for only two players to play through the game's story.

The overall tone of Tri Force Heroes is a comical one. The game rarely takes itself seriously, with characters having bizarre motivations and even stranger outfits. A man out in front of the game's main castle wears half an outfit, and the princess in need of "saving" cannot wear fancy clothes, which is why she needs a hero. There is also a pink-haired soldier who stands in front of the castle who looks remarkably similar to Link from Link to the Past. He is upset because he cannot pursue his own attempts to save the princess.

The Story

The land of Hytopia is proud of its many costumes. A witch, known only as The Lady, seeks out Hyoptia's Princess Styla,

and curses her to wear a plain black jumpsuit that she cannot take off or cover up.

In response, Styla's father, King Tuft, puts out a call for heroes to enter the Drablands to undo the curse. Link, who is traveling by Hytopia, takes on the challenge.

The Items

The items of Tri Force Heroes are your standard Zelda items, with many of the ones from Link Between Worlds making an appearance. The costumes, however, offer many different ways to play by offering bonuses for choosing to wear them into the Drablands.

Link works with the character Madame Couture to craft new outfits from assorted materials, and also finds them during his Drablands journeys.

Some highlights include wearing Zelda's dress, which causes hearts to appear more frequently. The Cacto Clothes make it look like Link is wearing a cactus and enemies who touch him automatically receive damage. The Goron Garb makes Link look like a Goron and fire cannot harm him.

All in all, including costumes that were added to the game after release in the form of downloadable updates, there are more than 35 costumes Link can wear.

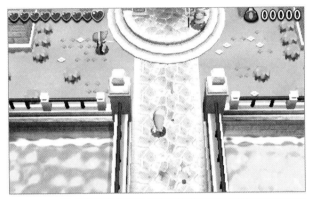

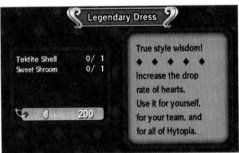

CHAPTER 20

The Legend of Zelda: Breath of the Wild (Switch, 2017)

First announced in 2013, Breath of the Wild began its life as a Wii U game before becoming the premiere launch title of Nintendo's newest console, the Switch. In the years prior, Zelda series producer Eiji Aonuma expressed an interest in looking at Zelda's core mechanics and changing them. Aonuma wanted players to be able to take dungeons out of order, play with others, and generally approach Zelda from a whole new direction. Some of these ideas can be seen in 2015's Tri Force Heroes, as well as 2013's A Link Between Worlds, but it is with Breath of the Wild that Zelda truly broke out of its comfort zone to become a wholly new experience that retained the exploratory feeling of a Zelda game, but without its increasingly familiar mechanics.

In Breath of the Wild, players are given an unprecedented level of freedom. Link can climb any surface, fall from any height, and literally fly using his paraglider. He is given a few suggestions for which direction to pursue, but everything is open to the players' preferences. If they want to aimlessly explore Hyrule, that's okay. Nothing is gated. If you just want to cook and collect food, or find horses, you can. If they want to go directly to

Ganon without solving any of the game's dungeons, they can. Every direction is open to the player after completing the first area.

Ambiguous from its opening moments, Breath of the Wild's story follows a different flow than previous Zelda games. Link wakes from a chamber that seems more electronic than magic, and is told by Zelda (heard for the first time in a Zelda game) that he has been asleep for 100 years and that Ganon must be defeated. From there, Link has to figure out why he was asleep and how to defeat Ganon.

Unlike the previous core console Zelda game, Skyward Sword, Breath of the Wild rarely locks players into long cutscenes, relying instead on the player to select which elements of the story he or she thinks are important. Breath of the Wild's story is entirely optional. Cutscenes reward finding and completing dungeons, and are also attached to a series of hidden moments throughout the world of Hyrule, but you do not need to see any of them in order to defeat Ganon. This is atypical not only for a Zelda game, but for all video games. It is totally up to the player how much story they're interested in seeing. Why Link has been asleep for as long as he has been, and why Ganon poses a constant and ever-present threat to the world becomes clear after playing the game, but it is entirely possible for a player to never learn why Link has been asleep for 100 years, and still see the game's final credits.

Breath of the Wild is the first Zelda game to feature voiced characters. It's also one of the only Zelda games that does not let the player select Link's name, since it is spoken by characters in assorted cutscenes. Zelda has a voice for the first time and speaks to Link throughout the game. In specific cutscenes, characters speak, and during dungeons you will also receive spoken tips and dialogue cues from an assortment of helpful characters. Nintendo has long held out on including voice performance in its games, citing that recorded dialogue means less opportunity for last-second changes to the game's story and dialogue. Not every line of dialogue is spoken in Breath of the Wild, but the important moments are. Shortly after the game's release, Nintendo released a patch for the game allowing players to play the game in any language they choose with any subtitle they choose, meaning if players wanted

to play and hear the game in its native language, Japanese, they could set it to be played that way with English subtitles.

Link finds all of the items he needs to use throughout the course of his adventure before leaving the opening area. Opposed to the typical Zelda items designed for solving puzzles in dungeons, Link uses a set of Runes, each with a distinct power. Normally, Link would find comparable items through the course of the game, each acquisition marking new level of progress, but in Breath of the Wild, Link has everything he needs

before leaving the opening Great Plateau area.

The Magnesis Rune lets Link move metal objects with a magnet. It has a number of applications, like moving giant metal tablets to create bridges, or lifting metal swords from beneath the water. The Magenesis Rune can also be used to pull open metal doors, or lift giant metal objects into the air in order to drop them on enemies.

The Remote Bomb Rune lets Link remotely detonate bombs and is about the closest Breath of the Wild has to a typical Zelda item. In the past, Link has always had

to collect bombs and keep an inventory of them in stock, but here, bombs are infinite. In a small, but undeniably brilliant game design mechanic, Link can choose between two different bomb shapes. The sphere bombs can roll a great distance and are perfect for placing at the top of a hill above an unsuspecting collection of enemies below. The cube-shaped bombs stay in place where you drop them, much more handy for use in puzzle solving. Link can also drop and explode bombs while gliding from his paraglider.

The Cryonis Rune creates giant blocks of ice in water that Link can stand on, but it has more applications than that. In puzzle solving, it allows Link to lift gates with water running underneath them. The Cryonis Rune can also be used to stop jets of water from spraying. Early in the game, before Link has more stamina, the Cryonis Rune can also be used to create a series of platforms across long stretches of water. This is a particularly handy skill when it comes to reaching faraway islands.

The Stasis Rune is one of the more difficult items to describe, but is also one of the most invaluable. It allows Link to stop time on certain objects and hit them in order to apply force to them while they are stopped in time. If an enemy is being particularly troublesome, Link can use the Rune to pause them and attack. If a giant boulder is rolling toward Link, he can pause it to get out of its way. If there is an explosive barrel just outside of an enemy encampment, Link can pause it with his Stasis Rune, hit it a few times with his sword, and then when it unpauses after a few moments, it will fly off into the distance and explode.

Finally, one the game's most useful items is the paraglider, which Link can use to glide from any height. Link receives the paraglider from a mysterious old man shortly after finding all the Runes and it opens up exploration in a profound way. It means no height is too high for Link, and huge distances can be covered in a short amount of time. Nothing is quite as rewarding as climbing to a great height, and taking a flying leap and pulling out your paraglider to fly off into the distance.

Outside of the Runes and paraglider, there are dozens of different swords, hammers, staffs, boomerangs, shields, and bow and arrows that can be collected throughout the game. Link never holds onto any of them for too long, however, as each is destructible and breaks after a few uses. It's one of the game's most controversial mechanics. On the one hand, losing a preferred weapon after only taking on a few enemies with it is disappointing, but constantly trying out new weapons and finding new ones as you explore is hugely rewarding. Whether or not this is an improvement to Zelda depends entirely on who you ask.

Breath of the Wild only has four core dungeons, a small number compared to Zeldas past, but it more than makes up for it with all the Shrines that litter its huge open world. The Shrines serve multiple purposes and act as miniature dungeons. Their main purpose is to act as fast-travel points for Link. You don't even have to complete a Shrine in order for it to become a fast-travel point, you just have to find it. They also serve to upgrade Link. Every Shrine rewards a Spirit Orb and Link can turn in Spirit Orbs for health or stamina upgrades. The challenges of the Shrines are diverse, but the majority of them are puzzle-based. Link must use his Runes in order to open doors or hit switches, or complete any number of

other puzzle-based tasks. Some Shrines are tests of strength, and Link must combat a powerful Guardian enemy inside them. Some Shrines instantly reward Link with a Spirit Orb as soon as he enters them, but those Shrines are often difficult to get to, or require some sort of task to be performed outside of the Shrine before they can be entered. Shrines offer some of the most interesting and varied challenges of the game and each is interesting in its own way.

Link can also cook, for the first time in a Zelda game, using ingredients found throughout the environment. Link can cook meats, or vegetarian dishes, or even fry up monster parts to create potions at the many assorted cooking stations littered throughout the game's world.

Beginner's Tips

Zelda's difficulty has never been consistent. Early Zelda games are difficult, and later games arguably hold the player's hand too much. Breath of the Wild finds a nice middle ground, offering a difficult challenge, especially in its early stages, but becomes easier as you get stronger. If you're playing Breath of the Wild for the first time, here are some tips to hopefully help you die less during your early hours.

Don't get too attached to weapons

As soon as they're about to break, throw them. A thrown weapon, even one that is about to break, does double the damage, and there is always a stronger weapon right around the corner.

Cook hearty meals

Many of the cooking items you will find in Hyrule will contain the word "heart" in their description, like the hearty trout, or the hearty turnip. Cooking these types of items

Seek out the Shrines

Every four Shrines Link finds and completes in Hyrule's open world give him the option to upgrade his stamina or his heart containers. Whenever you're up high, look for Shrines and mark their locations on your map, which brings up more tips.

Mark your map

It's up to the player to fill their map with icons and it's a good idea to do so. If you see unreachable chests, or a find a place with lots of great vegetables, mark it on

together will award Link plenty of extra hearts, which is especially helpful when you don't have many early in the game.

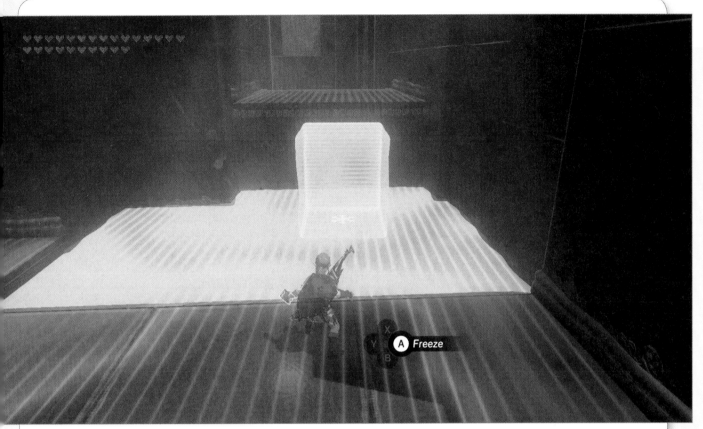

your map. Same goes for stores and other oddities seen in the world. You won't remember where everything is, so write it down.

Choose stamina over heart containers

Hearts mean you can take more hits, which is a tempting bonus when it comes to turning in your Shrines, but stamina is much more valuable. Lots of dishes will give you extra hearts, but it is harder to generate extra stamina with cooked dishes. Stamina

lets you climb higher, fly longer, and run longer, which is hugely important.

Don't turn off motion controls

Motion controls are often an annoyance, but they are used sparingly in Breath of the Wild. They really only come into play while aiming. Leaving motion controls on let you really dial in head-shots with precision. I would recommend at least trying them before running to the settings menu.

Collect arrows

Arrows are surprisingly rare, and surprisingly powerful in Breath of the Wild. Early in the game, a good way to build up a bank of them is to run in a circle as Bokoblins fire them at you. When they miss, you can grab their arrows from the ground.

Talk to everyone, especially the painter

It's always a good idea to talk to everyone who doesn't try to attack you first in a Zelda game, and Breath of the Wild is no exception. One of the most useful characters to talk to is a painter who often hangs out around stables. If you want to see all the story Breath of the Wild has to offer, he is the one to talk to.

Head northwest for your first dungeon

Breath of the Wild is designed in such a way where any dungeon can be played in any order, but arguably the best one to complete first is the one in the northwest. Every dungeon offers Link a powerful bonus, but the reward for completing that particular dungeon is arguably the most useful.

The Development

Development on Breath of the Wild began in earnest in 2013 after completing work on The Legend of Zelda: A Link Between Worlds. Nintendo wanted to make a much more open Zelda

and the first time it was brought to Nintendo mastermind and Zelda creator Shigeru Miyamoto, it was just a large open area with a handful of trees for Link to climb. The game's director, Hidemaro Fujibayashi, felt confident in his team's early concepts when Miyamoto was already having fun simply walking around and climbing trees.

At the annual Game Developer's Conference in 2017, Fujibayashi and key members of the game's development staff held a presentation titled Breaking Conventions with The Legend of Zelda: Breath of the Wild. In its presentation, Fujibayashi described the many strange directions Breath of the Wild nearly went in the team's efforts to break the Zelda formula. Early concept art showed radically different directions, like a moody one-armed Link who could create weapons and tools in place of his missing arm. They also showed a more cartoonish Link wearing jeans, wearing a spacesuit, and riding a motorcycle. Nintendo was open to any and all ideas. One idea that went beyond simply concept art and even became a playable demo, showed Link running across an open, war-torn field as he narrowly dodged laser blasts. This would eventually morph into the game's many battles with the Guardian enemies. Though not entirely new to Zelda, as he did encounter something similar in Majora's Mask, Nintendo even played with the idea of Link encountering an alien invasion.

One of the most interesting byproducts of the game's development, was a 2D version of the game that Nintendo used to lay out its world and play with all of its systems, like weather and fire, in a simplified form. Nintendo has not indicated that it has any intentions to release this game in any form, but it did show it briefly in action during the presentation.

Following the panel, Nintendo also released a

pair of videos documenting the game's development, where it discussed in more detail assorted inspirations for the game, as well as elements that did not make the final cut. One of the more substantial cuts in the game was an area with a tiny village full of miniature Minish-like people. The game's art director, Satoru Takizawa, said the inspiration for the game's technology and its Shiekah people come from the Jōmon period of Japanese history. The game's director also cited Kyoto, Japan, the city in

which the game was developed, as a major inspiration for the general layout of Hyrule.

In another unprecedented development idea, not just for Zelda, but for all video games, Nintendo said all through the game's development, even leading up to its final months, when most studios would be scrambling to finish the game, Nintendo would take off full weeks for the team to just play the game and really hone in on what works and what is fun.

Wii U versus Nintendo Switch

On the same day Breath of the Wild released on Nintendo's new console, the Switch, the game also released on Wii U. In 2013, when Breath of the Wild was first revealed, it was shown running on Wii U hardware and it was always meant to be a Wii U game. It was well in development before the decision was made to bring the game to Switch.

The Wii U version of the game is identical in nearly all ways, except for its resolution and sound quality. The Switch version of the game runs at a 900p resolution when played on a TV, while the Wii U version runs at 720p. The sound of the Switch version is also slightly better than the Wii U version of the game, but only by a little bit.

In early builds of the Wii U version of the game, inventory management and other details were handled on the game's second GamePad screen, but for its final release, these mechanics were removed, presumably, to make the game identical to its Switch counterpart.

The Reception

The Legend of Zelda: Breath of the Wild was a colossal critical and commercial success. Currently, it holds the record for most perfect review scores on Metacritic.com, a website that gathers review scores from many different outlets. It also, impossibly, sold more Switch copies than Nintendo sold Switch consoles. According to Nintendo, this is due to many players buying a collector's edition of game to keep, and one regular edition to play.

Breath of the Wild marked a brave new direction for the Zelda series. It undeniably feels like a Zelda game, but shares surprisingly little with the previous entries.

Even only a matter of months after its launch on Switch, some fans were calling it the best Zelda game ever, and even the best game, period. Time will tell where it falls in the history of the series, and how it will influence the games that come after it, but there is no denying that Nintendo's bold experiment with Zelda was a huge success.

CHAPTER 21

The Legend of Zelda Timeline

Almost all Zelda games feature their own story, and aren't connected to the game that came before it. Some of the games are direct sequels, like the first two Zeldas, or Wind Waker and Phantom Hourglass, but for the most part, every Link and every Zelda have their own one-off adventures.

Fans of the series always assumed the Zelda games represented an ongoing war between good and evil, where a boy named Link and a girl named Zelda would appear every few generations to fight a man named Ganon. Nintendo was quiet about this idea for years, but in 2011, that changed.

Nintendo published a book called *Hyrule Historia* that celebrated the series and featured the art for each entry in the series. One of the most interesting aspects of *Hyrule Historia*, however, was the official Zelda timeline. It places each Zelda game at a specific point in time and confirmed a long-debated fan theory about the existence of multiple timelines.

The debate over the timeline has shifted in recent years away from whether or not it exists, to whether or not Nintendo had a timeline in mind for Zelda since the beginning of the first game. It's unlikely we will learn the true answer to that question any time soon, but in the meantime, we do know in what order the games take place.

The Legend of Zelda: Skyward Sword

Before the game was even released, Nintendo was clear that Skyward Sword was meant to be the first game in the Zelda timeline. At the end of the game, Link and Zelda choose to leave their home in Skyloft in order to establish the kingdom of Hyrule on the ground below.

The Legend of Zelda: The Minish Cap

This story establishes why the legendary hero wears a green hat, and also introduces the evil wizard Vaati.

The Legend of Zelda: Four Swords

Not to be confused with the GameCube game, Four Swords Adventures, Four Swords is the bonus game included with A Link to the Past's Game Boy Advance port. In the game, Link and Zelda continue their fight against Vaati.

The Legend of Zelda: Ocarina of Time

Ocarina of Time introduces the legacy of the Hero of Time, and also marks a very complicated three-way split in Zelda's timeline. This is where things get complicated.

Link's time-traveling adventures in Ocarina created multiple timelines, each offering distinct futures. There are three ways Ocarina of Time conceivably ends, and the first is if Link loses to Ganondorf.

The first timeline

When the Hero of Time loses to Ganondorf, the world is plunged into darkness and war, until…

The Legend of Zelda: A Link to the Past

Ganon is brought back to life, but Link and Zelda are able to banish him again.

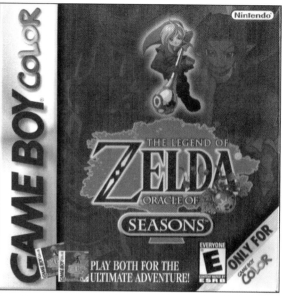

The Legend of Zelda: Oracle of Ages and Time

This is the same Link that appeared in Link to the Past, and he and Zelda successfully prevent another Ganon awakening. The game actually ends with Link going out to sea…

The Legend of Zelda: Link's Awakening

…and crashing on Koholint Island. It seems like everything that happens in this game is all a dream, but even if that is the case, the Link from A Link to the Past and the Oracle games did at the very least make his way out to sea and get caught in a storm.

The Legend of Zelda: A Link Between Worlds

A Link Between World's placement in the timeline cannot be confirmed by *Hyrule Historia*, but it recognizes the legacy of Link to the Past in-game and treats it as a legend from hundreds of years ago.

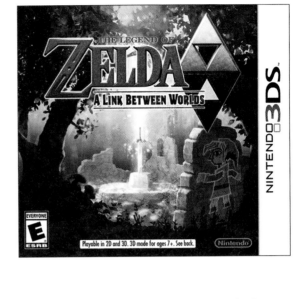

The Legend of Zelda: Tri Force Heroes

Nintendo has stated that the Link who appears in A Link Between Worlds is the same Link as Tri Force Heroes, which places it here in the timeline.

The Legend of Zelda

Even though it's the first Zelda game, it appears very late in the timeline. Technically, Ganon had been brought back to life and re-banished multiple times by this point.

Zelda II: The Adventure of Link

As the sequel to the original Zelda that features the same Link, Zelda II fits here.

The second timeline

If we go back to Ocarina of Time, there are other timelines to examine. We looked at one where Link loses. This is the timeline where child Link gets to start over.

The Legend of Zelda: Majora's Mask

Following the events of Ocarina of Time, Link gets to actually live out his childhood, but he chooses to leave home in search of Navi and gets caught up in an adventure.

The Legend of Zelda: Twilight Princess

This marks another jump of hundreds of years, where the Shadow World begins to invade Hyrule in an attempt to bring Ganon back to life. He comes back to life, but only briefly as Link and Zelda are able to stop him.

The Link of Twilight Princess learns new techniques from an ancient spirit simply called the Ancient Hero. Though never said in the game, many think that this Ancient Hero is in fact Link from Ocarina of Time teaching a new generation how to fight.

The Legend of Zelda: Four Swords Adventures

This is another big jump that recalls the Picori legends as well as the return of Vaati, who has proven himself to be a villain for Link through the centuries.

The third timeline

Back to Ocarina of Time, again. We've seen the timeline if Link loses and the one where child Link continues his journey. This third timeline is what happens when adult Link is not given the chance to go back to his childhood.

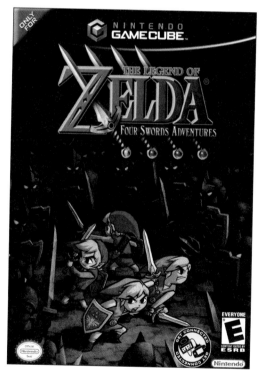

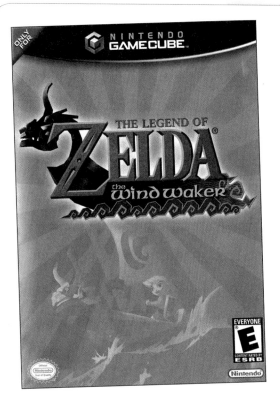

The Legend of Zelda: The Wind Waker

Hundreds of years after the events of Ocarina of Time, Ganon is back and no hero appears to stop him, which floods the world of Hyrule. Ganon is much older than Link in The Wind Waker, and that's because his reign began with no hero to stop him. It is only later in his life that a hero appears.

The Legend of Zelda: Phantom Hourglass

One of the few Zelda games that is actually a sequel. This continues the adventures of the Link and Zelda from Wind Waker.

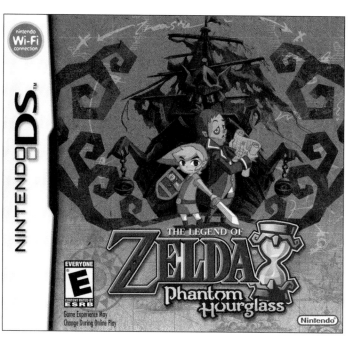

The Legend of Zelda: Spirit Tracks

Hundreds of years pass, the world's flooding subsides, and a new Hyrule is established. Also, train technology emerges.

The Legend of Zelda: Breath of the Wild

Breath of the Wild, the youngest of the Zelda games, has no confirmed spot on the Zelda timeline. Some think it represents the three timelines merging back together, since it contains reference to Zelda games across all three timelines. Others think it takes place many thousands of years after the events of Spirit Tracks. Every Zelda fan seems to have a different theory about where Breath of the Wild belongs on the timeline, and even though nearly every theory is different, everyone is certain they are correct.

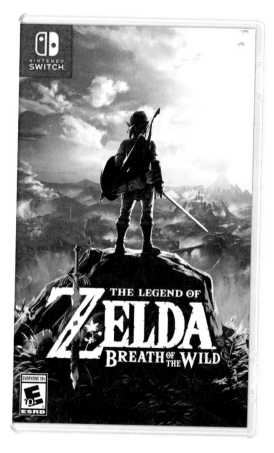

Nintendo®

The Legend of
ZELDA®

**GAME WATCH
BY NELSONIC**

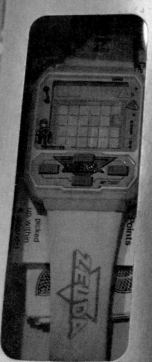

4-41112

Nintendo®

The Legend of
ZELDA®

GAME WATCH

- Designed after the home video game
- Keeps score, records higher score
- The Legend of Zelda Characters
- Quartz accuracy
- Sporty case and band
- Battery included
- Daily Alarm

© 1989 NINTENDO OF AMERICA, INC.

Official
Nintendo®
Licensed Product

CHAPTER 22

The Spinoffs and Guest Appearances

Not every Zelda game is a complete adventure, or even directly related to the Zelda universe. These are the games that are in some way connected to Zelda, or use the Zelda name, but are not considered a real part of the Zelda universe.

The Legend of Zelda Watches

In 1989, Nintendo released two small LCD games based on Zelda. One was part of Nintendo's Game and Watch line, which ported assorted Nintendo games to a limited, dual-screen LCD handheld. In the game, Link must defeat eight dragons to rescue Princess Zelda.

The Legend of Zelda Game Watch made the game even smaller, so players could wear the game on their wrist. In that game, players defeat enemies in order to collect and reassemble the Triforce.

The Philips CD-i Games

These are definitely the strangest of the spinoff Zelda bunch. In 1991, Nintendo was

working with Philips to create a CD-ROM add-on for the Super Nintendo. The add-on never came to be, but as a result of the process, Philips was able to use a few of Nintendo's characters in games for its own console, the Philips CD-i.

Philips produced four games using Nintendo's characters. One was a game called Hotel Mario, but the other three were Zelda games.

Link: The Faces of Evil

The first of the Philips Zelda games, this one features Link collecting items in the game, but that's about where the comparisons to

Zelda end. It's a side-scrolling game, and features weird animated scenes with strange voiceovers.

Zelda: The Wand of Gamelon

The Wand of Gamelon is the first game that lets you play as the character the game is actually named after. Zelda collects items and uses them as Link did in Faces of Evil, and features the same side-scrolling gameplay and strange animated scenes.

Zelda's Adventure

In Zelda's Adventure you continue to play as Zelda, but the gameplay is more like

Nintendo's Zelda games. You view the action from an overhead perspective. The animated scenes were dropped in favor of using live-action actors.

Freshly-Picked Tingle's Rosy Rupeeland

Tingle, a character introduced in Majora's Mask, went on to become a fan favorite. He's a strange, overly optimistic man in a green leotard who went on to appear in Wind Waker and in Minish Cap.

Freshly-Picked Tingle's Rosy Rupeeland was his first starring role. In the game, Tingle

collects Rupees and explores the world surrounding his home, helping those in need and fighting enemies while trying to collect a large fortune.

The game was never released in North America, but it did receive a full English translation for a European release. European DS cartridges can be played in North American DS handhelds making it a relatively easy game to track down and play.

Link's Crossbow Training

About a year after the launch of the Wii, Nintendo released a special add-on called the Wii Zapper. The Zapper was a plastic shell players could insert the Wii Remote and Nunchuck into to make the controller function like a gun and improve accuracy.

The Zapper came bundled with a copy of Link's Crossbow Training. Crossbow Training uses Twilight Princess' art style for a shooting gallery game. It features no true story, and instead just offers a series of shooting challenges for players to enjoy.

Hyrule Warriors

Hyrule Warriors is a big celebration of the Zelda franchise, and surprisingly did not come from Nintendo. Nintendo oversaw the project, but it was actually developed in a joint effort by Omega Force and Team Ninja. Omega Force is known for the historical action game series Dynasty Warriors, and Omega Force is known for the Ninja Gaiden series of games.

Hyrule Warriors does not fit into the Zelda timeline, and instead visits many of its most famous moments and characters, mashing them all together into one big action-focused Zelda experience.

The game's plot is just an excuse to have an assortment of Zelda characters meet and fight together. The game plays out like a war with the player character fighting hundreds of enemies at a time on big open fields.

The game features more than 25 playable characters, each with an assortment of costumes. Three different versions of Link are playable, and there is even a character named Linkle that imagines Link as a female character. Zelda is playable in multiple forms, as are many of Zelda's villains. Even more obscure characters like Medli from Wind Waker and Marin from Link's Awakening (seen in 3D for the first time) were also added to the game as downloadable content after the game was released.

The game also includes a special adventure mode that recalls the original Zelda by letting players explore the original pixelated version of the map, while playing through combat scenarios to unlock items.

It doesn't feel like a Zelda game, because it's all about the action, but it's a fun way to celebrate the action side of the Zelda series.

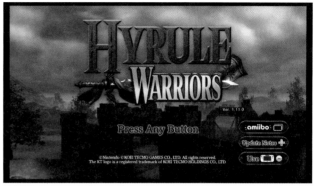

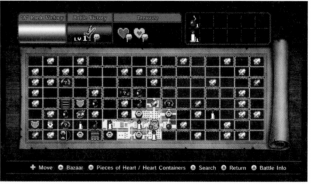

My Nintendo Picross— The Legend of Zelda: Twilight Princess

Picross is a long-running puzzle franchise for Nintendo. It's a series that has been around since the Game Boy with Mario's Picross. In the game, players solve logic puzzles to create pictures.

My Nintendo Picross—The Legend of Zelda: Twilight Princess was a promotional game players could earn for free by participating in its My Nintendo program, where you earn points for playing and buying Nintendo games. All of the game's puzzles are themed around Zelda, specifically Twilight Princess.

Only in Japan

With a few exceptions, the Zelda games were usually released in Japan first. Here are a few titles that never made their way to North America, and likely never will.

Zelda no Densetsu: Kamigami no Triforce (Barcode Battler II)

This game was a simple RPG featuring Link to the Past characters and enemies. It was for a console called the Barcode Battler II, a handheld system that was never released in North America. With the Barcode Battler, players could swipe special cards to unlock and play with assorted characters. Nintendo released a few Zelda cards for the system based on Link to the Past.

BS Zelda no Densetsu

In 1995, Nintendo released the Satellaview for the Super Nintendo in Japan. It allowed games to be broadcast from a satellite and received by players at home. This was many years before the Internet made downloading games easy.

The BS part of the title in BS Zelda no Densetsu stands for "Broadcast Satellite." Nintendo broadcast this Zelda game on the platform and it was sort of an enhanced version of the original Zelda. The game was playable only at certain times between 1995 and 1997, and the technology allowed for it to have spoken dialogue—a first for a Zelda game.

The game did not star Link, and instead players took on the role of the character they selected when they set up their Satellaview. The game is not currently playable, due to the strange and eventually abandoned satellite technology.

BS Zelda no Densetsu: Inishie no Sekiban

This Satellaview game was, in some ways, an enhanced version of Link to the Past. It was broadcast in 1997 and featured spoken dialogue. Like the previous game, players played as their Satellaview character instead of Link and it featured an original story. It is also no longer playable, like BS Zelda no Densetsu.

Tingle's Balloon Fight

Balloon Fight is a classic 1980s Nintendo game where players have to fly through a sky full of obstacles while attached to floating balloons. In 2007, Nintendo released a version of Balloon Fight starring Tingle just for Club Nintendo members. When players met Tingle in Majora's Mask, he is seen floating in the air attached to a balloon, making him a good fit for this game.

Dekisugi Tingle Pack

This wasn't so much a game as much as it was a series of Tingle-themed applications for use on the DSi. The pack featured a timer, calculator, music program, fortune teller, and coin game.

Irozuki Tincle no Koi no Balloon Trip

The title roughly translates to "Ripening Tingle's Balloon Trip of Love," and is a sequel to Freshly-Picked Tingle's Rosy Rupeeland. It was only released in Japan, and was a big hit. It features Tingle exploring a mysterious world with three partners who are essentially the Scarecrow, the Tin Woodman, and the Cowardly Lion from The Wizard of Oz.

Guest Appearances

Link and other characters from the Zelda universe have appeared in other games, though not that often, especially when compared to Nintendo's other characters, like Mario.

Super Smash Bros.

When Super Smash Bros. was released on Nintendo 64, Nintendo was no stranger to using its cast of characters in various party games. But no characters from the Zelda franchise had ever appeared in another game until Super Smash Bros., which featured Link.

Super Smash Bros. Melee

The sequel to Super Smash Bros. expanded Zelda's role by including Link, young Link (specifically the Ocarina of Time version),

Zelda and Sheik (as a single character able to switch roles mid-battle), and Ganondorf.

Soul Calibur II

In 2003 the popular fighting game Soul Calibur decided to include a special exclusive guest character based on the

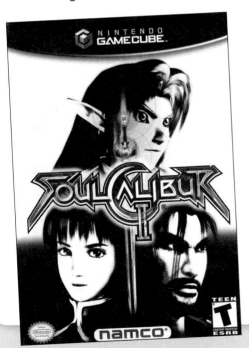

platform you were playing on. The Xbox version got the comic book character Spawn. The PlayStation 2 version of the game got Heihachi, from the fighting series Tekken. And the GameCube got Link. Many considered Link to be an overpowered fighter in Soul Calibur II, but everyone appreciated seeing him make an appearance in the game.

Super Smash Bros. Brawl

For the third Smash Bros. game, the Zelda cast mostly appeared as they usually did. Link, the Zelda/Sheik character, and Ganondorf were mostly unchanged. Young Link, however, was swapped for Toon Link from The Legend of Zelda: The Wind Waker.

Mario Kart 8

Up until this point, Link and his friends had stuck to fighting games. After the release of Mario Kart 8, however, Nintendo announced

Super Smash Bros. 3DS

The fourth Super Smash Bros. also released on 3DS and included the same roster of Zelda fighters, but had some cool bonuses, like a fighting arena based on The Legend of Zelda: Spirit Tracks.

plans to release a Zelda track for the game, and make Link a playable racer.

He must be bought separately, but adding Link to Mario Kart 8 also adds a series of Zelda-themed kart pieces, and the Hyrule Circuit track, which takes racers through Hyrule Castle. Another nice little touch is that instead of collecting coins on the Zelda track, racers pick up rupees.

Super Smash Bros. Wii U

The big change for Smash Bros. number four, in terms of Zelda character appearances, was that Sheik and Zelda were separate characters.

Unreleased Games

It's incredibly rare that a Zelda game is publicly unveiled and never releases, but there are a few examples. Some were announced games that simply never released, while some were never meant to be released games, but were instead technical demos shared with the public.

The Legend of Zelda: Mystical Seed of Courage

When the Oracle of Ages and Seasons games were initially being planned, there was originally a third game, Mystical Seed of Courage. Plans for the game were abandoned supposedly due to problems making the three games interact, but had it released, it would have featured oracle Farore and its key mechanic would have been connected to the time of day.

Uru Zelda

Planned as an expansion of sorts for Ocarina of Time, the game was meant to be released for the 64DD expansion drive. The 64DD was an add-on for the Nintendo 64 that increased its processing power, but it never released in North America, and was considered a commercial failure in Japan. Uru Zelda was canceled when Nintendo stopped support for the 64DD.

Supposedly, the expansion was meant to dramatically change the overworld of Ocarina of Time, change the dungeons, and introduce new enemies. It later released in a form without new dungeons, new enemies, or a changed overworld, with the Ocarina of Time Master Quest. That version of the game was offered as a pre-order bonus for fans who pre-purchased Wind Waker, and was also unlockable in the 3DS version of Ocarina of Time.

The Legend of Zelda: Spaceworld 2000 Demo

In 2000 at Nintendo's formerly annual Spaceworld conference, the company attempted to generate enthusiasm for its upcoming GameCube console by showcasing a short video of Link and Ganondorf, modeled after their Ocarina of Time versions, embroiled in a sword fight using the GameCube's graphical capabilities. The assumption was that it was a teaser for the next Zelda for release on GameCube, but it never came to be.

The Legend of Zelda Wii U

Well before the unveiling of Breath of the Wild, Nintendo used The Legend of Zelda to help sell the potential of the Wii U. It prepared a somewhat playable demo of a Zelda game using its new console. In the demo, a realistic Link with a fairy companion entered a dungeon and encountered a gigantic spider enemy. Link moved on his own, but players could control the camera and change the game's lighting. Nintendo was explicit early on that it was never meant to be a new Zelda game, and was instead created purely to show off the Wii U's technical potential.

COLLECTOR'S EDITION
THE LEGEND OF
ZELDA®
The Complete Season
Over 3 Hours of Action
THE LEGEND OF ZELDA
The Complete Season

CHAPTER 23

The Multimedia and Merchandise of The Legend of Zelda

The Legend of Zelda mostly sticks to video games, but it has ventured beyond the bounds of interactive media on a few occasions.

The Legend of Zelda TV Series

In 1989, a show called The Super Mario Bros. Super Show! aired on television. It starred a live-action Mario and Luigi (Lou Albano and Danny Wells, respectively) as they interacted with guest stars and dealt with problems, usually related to plumbing.

Those live-action segments were used to introduce animated episodes of Super Mario Bros., but once a week, the segment would be replaced by an animated show based on The Legend of Zelda.

The show mostly followed the original two games, and starred Zelda and Link as they fought Ganon and defended Hyrule. A fairy character named Spryte would also typically be part of each episode.

Link speaks in the show and has a sarcastic sense of humor. He also had a catchphrase. He was always trying to get a kiss from Zelda as a reward for his heroics, but she always turned him down, to which he would reply, "Well, excuuuuuse me, Princess."

Zelda was far from a damsel in distress in the show, often fighting alongside Link with a bow and arrow in their efforts to defeat Ganon.

The show was goofy, didn't look much like the games, and was canceled after 13 episodes alongside the cancellation of The Super Mario Bros. Super Show! The animated series is available on DVD today.

Captain N: The Game Master

Captain N aired around the same time as The Super Mario Bros. Super Show! and featured all kinds of cameos from video game characters. The show follows a boy named Kevin Keene, who gets sucked into the world of Videoland, where he is to become Captain N: The Game Master.

The show featured a cast of video game characters, like Simon Belmont from Castlevania, Kid Icarus, and Mega Man, but Zelda characters do make minor appearances.

Link, Zelda, and Ganon all appear in multiple episodes, and Kevin names Link his favorite video game character. Though

airing around the same time as the animated Zelda series, Link is older in Captain N, and is not as goofy and sarcastic.

The Legend of Zelda Graphic Novels

In Japan, nearly every Zelda game has received a comic book adaptation, but not all of them have been translated for release in North America. Most of them have been written and drawn by two women who go by the joint name Akira Himekawa.

Himekawa has written and drawn comics based on a Link to the Past, Ocarina of Time, Majora's Mask, Oracle of Ages and Seasons, Four Swords, Minish Cap, Twilight Princess, Phantom Hourglass, and Skyward Sword.

In 1990, an American company, Valiant Comics, released a series of Zelda comics that expanded the history of the games. They were written by George Caragonne and adopted the art style established by the animated show.

In 1992, Nintendo Power magazine published a comic that served as a retelling of Link to the Past written by Shotaro Ishinomori. Ishinomori is well known in Japan for his creation Cyborg 009. Simply titled The Legend of Zelda: A Link to the Past, Ishinomori's comic was recently collected and re-published.

The Choose Your Own Adventure Books

In addition to comic books, Nintendo also created a few Choose Your Own Adventure books. In 1992, Nintendo published two Zelda books titled The Crystal Trap and The Shadow Prince. In the books, readers are given choices from time to time and must skip to specific chapters based on their decisions. There is a correct ending, but many endings result in the defeat of the hero.

The Crystal Trap follows Zelda as she attempts to free Link from the trap in just 24 hours. The Shadow Prince focuses on Link as he attempts to save Zelda with the help of a mysterious hero named Charles.

In 2001, Nintendo released a new pair of Choose Your Own Adventure books to go alongside the release of Oracle of Ages and Oracle of Seasons. The two books follow the basic plots of their game versions.

Merchandise

It's not hard to find officially licensed merchandise based on The Legend of Zelda. You can get Zelda on everything from cereal to T-shirts to the very console you play the game on. In 1988, Nintendo sold a cereal that featured a Mario and Zelda cereal in the same box. Here are a few of the stand-out items.

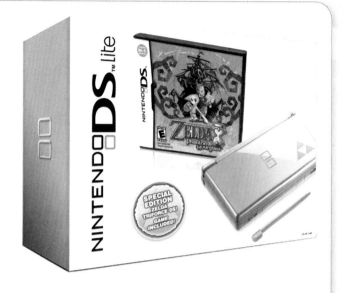

The Legend of Zelda Special Edition Consoles

Nintendo has, on occasion, commemorated the release of a new Zelda game or a Zelda anniversary with the release of a special edition Zelda console. These are typically released in limited quantities and are highly collectible.

GBA SP Zelda Gold

One of the first official Zelda special edition handheld consoles, the system is gold featuring a large Triforce on the outside, and a small Hylian Crest on the lower-right corner below the A and B buttons.

DS Lite Legend of Zelda: Phantom Hourglass Gold

Sold alongside the release of The Legend of Zelda: Phantom Hourglass, the Zelda DS Lite was gold and featured a Triforce decal.

3DS The Legend of Zelda

This early model 3DS was released alongside the 3DS remake of Ocarina of Time. Unlike most of the gold consoles on this list, this one is black with a golden Hylian Crest and decals around the edges with ocarinas and harps.

The other amiibo unlock weapons and clothes based on their specific appearances. For example, the Wind Waker Link amiibo sometimes awards the player an outfit based on The Wind Waker for Breath of the Wild Link to use in-game.

Monopoly: The Legend of Zelda Collector's Edition

Nintendo partnered with Hasbro for a Zelda-themed Monopoly board. All the spaces reflect the Zelda games and it comes with game pieces of the Triforce, the Hylian Shield, the bow, the slingshot, the hookshot, and the Gale Boomerang from Twilight Princess.

Figures and statues

Nintendo's amiibo are great figures, but there are plenty of others out there working with Nintendo to produce high-quality figures and statues.

First 4 Figures has a full collection of statues that can get very expensive. They cover the obvious figures, like the Links, Zeldas, and Ganondorfs, but also cover the more obscure characters, like Skull Kid and Majora's Mask.

Nendoroid and Figma figures are a product of the Japanese company Good Smile. They focus on figures based on anime, manga, video games, and have lots of high-quality Zelda figures. The Nendoroid figures often have unusual dimensions, and the Figma line of figures are often more realistic.

Good Smile has created Zelda and Link figures based on their Wind Waker looks, as well as a Link figure based on his Majora's Mask appearance. You can also find Figma figures of Zelda and Link from Twilight Princess, as well as Link from Skyward Sword, and a figure based on A Link Between Worlds' Link.

The Influence of The Legend of Zelda

The Legend of Zelda is a hugely influential game. The game and its many sequels offered a great sense of exploration, especially compared to other games of that generation. Mario inspired game creators to develop a series of games that were fun to play, containing challenges that players could work their way through. The Legend of Zelda offered a world players could explore the way they wanted to, creating an incredible sense of wonder.

Zelda presents problems to the player that cannot be solved right away. Later, when the player finds the tool they need to solve the problem they couldn't solve before, they are rewarded both by solving the puzzle and with the feeling that they are in control of the game. This is something that is seen is almost all games today.

Zelda also introduced the ability to save your game. Thanks to this option, Zelda was a game designed from the beginning to be an extended experience that could be played over a long period of time. It was a world players could return to, not one that would reset every time the player decided to play it. Saving is a crucial element of nearly all games today, but when Zelda was created there was nothing else like it.

The open-world game has become a hugely successful type of game today, and Zelda was one of the first games where players could take off in any direction they chose. The world felt like it continued to exist, even if you weren't looking directly at it. Today's open worlds look toward Zelda as the beginning of the open world concept, which is especially impressive considering it started out on an 8-bit console.

The player character in Zelda is named Link, but that doesn't have to be his name. Link can be called whatever you want him to be. Miyamoto wanted him to serve as a link between the player and the game, allowing players to give him their own personality, something which continues today for many games.

The very first Zelda had a secret second quest for players who entered their name as "Zelda." The very idea of an entire second quest existing, hidden in the game, made the world into something much bigger than players expected. This idea continued with many of the games featuring dark or alternate worlds.

The Games Directly Inspired by The Legend of Zelda

Many games can point toward The Legend of Zelda for some of its style or gameplay goals, but these games make no secret about their inspiration. They are highly original titles that separate themselves from The Legend of Zelda in meaningful ways, but there is no doubt that they would not exist if not for The Legend of Zelda.

Alundra

Alundra follows a character named Alundra, who crash lands on an island near a village called Inoa. Alundra has the power to enter people's dreams, and does so in order to help the locals of Inoa. He solves puzzles, fights with a sword, and it all takes place from the overhead perspective.

Beyond Good and Evil

Beyond Good and Evil the video game doesn't share a whole lot in common with the book of the same name by philosopher Friedrich Nietzsche, but it does share a lot with Zelda.

The game follows Jade, a reporter on her home planet of Hillys as she tries to uncover a government conspiracy that involves aliens. The game comes from Michel Ancel, the creator of Rayman, and feels like a Zelda game in many ways. It takes place in a large, open 3D world, and Jade must solve puzzles while collecting new items and fighting off the bad guys.

Okami

In Okami, players play as the sun goddess Amaterasu, as she tries to prevent the resurrection of a great evil. Created by Hideki Kamiya, who worked with Capcom on the Resident Evil and Devil May Cry series, Okami follows the standard Zelda structure, with some important twists.

Amaterasu makes her way through an open world with the aid of her companion and guide, Issun, solving puzzles and fighting evil. Instead of a sword, however, Amaterasu uses her celestial brush, which allows her to literally paint attacks on her enemies, and solve puzzles in the environment.

3D Dot Game Heroes

3D Dot Game Heroes looks specifically at the original Zelda on NES for inspiration. It is a world built with pixelated blocks, but with the lighting and special effects of a modern console.

In the game, players explore a large open world, fighting monsters, solving puzzles, and even collecting items like a boomerang and bow and arrow. It was definitely made by people who loved the original Zelda game.

Darksiders and Darksiders II

Darksiders was co-directed by Joe Madureira, a comic book artist known for his series Battle Chasers and his work on Uncanny X-men. Madureira left the comic book industry (at least for a while) to bring his vision for Darksiders to life.

In the game, players take on the role of War, a Horseman of the Apocalypse, as he tries to undo an apocalypse, which he has been accused of starting early. Clearing his name involves exploring dungeons and using an assortment of discovered items to solve puzzles.

Two years after its release, a sequel came out staring Death, another Horseman of the Apocalypse.

Among the games mentioned on this list, the Darksiders series is the most similar to Zelda, which is exactly what Madureira said he wanted to do.

Hyper Light Drifter

This 2016 independent game from developer Heart Machine was influenced specifically by the 2D Zelda games, and uses a pixelated art

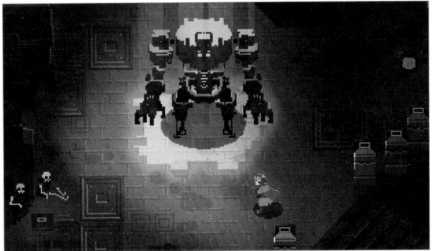

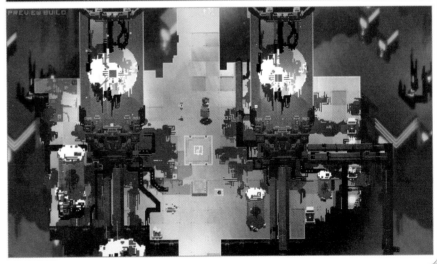

style reminiscent of the Super Nintendo. It uses the same overhead perspective as the 2D Zelda games, where players explore a large open world, fighting with a sword and discovering secrets in order to make themselves stronger.

The developer, Heath Machine, openly referenced The Legend of Zelda as inspiration, citing a desire to craft a game that offered the same sort of exploratory rewards as the original Zelda games.

Oceanhorn: Monster of Uncharted Seas

Oceanhorn is an unapologetic love letter to The Legend of Zelda. It draws directly from The Wind Waker for its open-ocean world, as well as the dungeon and action gameplay of A Link to the Past. In the games, players explore an ocean, discover dungeons with puzzles, and fight with a sword while keeping an eye on their heart meter.

The game's music was composed by renowned Final Fantasy composer, Nobuo Uematsu, which answered a question many Zelda and Final Fantasy fans had: what if Final Fantasy's composer wrote Zelda music?

CHAPTER 25

The Future of The Legend of Zelda

As the Legend of Zelda celebrates 30 years, it is difficult to say what the future of the franchise will hold. With the release of The Legend of Zelda: Breath of the Wild and its downloadable content, there is currently no upcoming Zelda game announced to be in the works. That, of course, does not mean one is not currently being planned by Nintendo. In all likelihood, work on the next big Zelda game has already begun in secret. Series producer Eiji Aonuma has already discussed in mysterious fashion what's next for Zelda.

The success of Breath of the Wild, as well as interviews with Aonuma, seem to hint that whatever future we can expect for Zelda, it will be sticking to the open-world philosophy it established for Breath of the Wild. He has also hinted that 2D Zelda games are still very much a part of the series' future, and in all likelihood, will appear on Nintendo's new console, the Switch. In recent years, 2D Zelda's have been relegated to handheld systems like the 3DS and Game Boy Advance, but since the Switch serves as both a mobile and home console platform, it's likely the

next 2D Zelda will appear on that console. We can make some simple assumptions about the next Zelda game—it will be open world, Link will probably have to save Zelda—but beyond that, where will the franchise go next? We're not sure.

Aonuma, pledged to rethink the franchise in 2013, which resulted in successful experiments like A Link Between Worlds and Breath of the Wild, where players could take its dungeons in any order they pleased, free of exploratory restriction. There's no guarantee Zelda will even continue to be a single-player experience, as demonstrated by Tri Force Heroes.

There have even been rumors of more multimedia adaptations of the Zelda franchise, with film and TV opportunities, and Nintendo has said it wants to leverage its cast of characters in more interesting ways. It's entirely possible we may see an official Zelda story exist outside of its video game adaptations sometime soon.

Nothing is guaranteed, but Zelda and its wider universe is in good hands with Nintendo. It created the world of Hyrule in 1986, but has frequently re-imagined the franchise, all without losing a continued sense of wonder and exploration.

Zelda is a prime example of what the interactive medium of storytelling is capable of achieving. It has continued to entertain and thrill players for 30 years. Players feel like they're a part of Hyrule and have a real impact on what happens in the world. These are not Link's adventure—they are our adventures.

After 30 years, more than 15 games, and many spinoffs, Zelda continues to be one of the most popular franchises in the video game industry. The number of Zelda fans, both young and old, continues to grow with each new entry and will very likely continue another 30 years, and even further into the future.